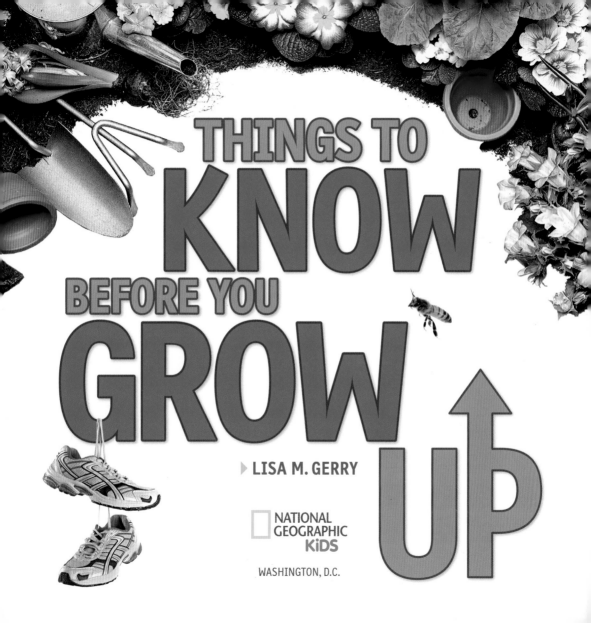

THINGS TO KNOW BEFORE YOU GROW UP

▶ LISA M. GERRY

NATIONAL
GEOGRAPHIC
KiDS

WASHINGTON, D.C.

Psssst. Hey, you!

Come on over—we've got a secret to share. Actually, more like **100 secrets!** Because beyond the spelling bees and long division of normal everyday life, there are a few things we think **you should know ... the _big_ stuff ...** like how to **make ice cream out of snow,** how to take a great school picture, or how to tell someone you _like_ like them.

This book is chock-full of the information you need to be the **best version of YOU.** You know, a normal kid but with **superhuman, super awesome skills** for dealing with tough times—like how to say "I'm sorry," how to recover from **embarrassment,** and what to do in an **emergency.** You'll even get to know yourself a bit better by learning how to be brave, how to relax, and how to pick yourself up when you're feeling down. And just for good measure, we've thrown in all kinds of really **fun and practical skills,** like how to pump up your bike tires, how to manage your money, and how to **plan a party.**

In these pages, there are interviews with **experts and explorers,** insider tips, and happy how-to's. There's even a handy to-do list, so you can keep track of all your accomplishments. So what are you waiting for? Go on now, and get excited. **You've got a lot to learn!**

100 things to know before you grow up? National Geographic wants you to know what explorers know, what makes them successful as they explore the world.

National Geographic explorers are curious, responsible, and empowered.

They have skills of observation, communication, collaboration, and problem-solving.

They know things about our human story, our living planet, critical species, and new frontiers.

Attitude

? Curiosity

♥ Responsibility

✊ Empowerment

Skills

👁 Observation

💬 Communication

⚙ Collaboration

💡 Problem-Solving

Knowledge

🚶 Our Human Story

🌱 Our Living Planet

🐘 Critical Species

🚀 New Frontiers

Look for these icons throughout the book coded to the 100 things. At the end, we'll tell you a little more about how to shout out your smarts and keep exploring.

how to

make

SNOW
ICE CREAM

Sick of snowmen? Tired of tubing? Take a break from your frosty snow day fun with this delicious treat!

Weird but true! EVEN THOUGH IT'S MADE OF SNOW, THE INSIDE OF AN IGLOO IS WARMED BY BODY HEAT AND CAN BE UP TO 100°F (56°C) WARMER THAN OUTSIDE.

STEP 1
Collect clean snow in a bowl.

STEP 2
Add sweetened condensed milk (or heavy cream and sugar) to taste.

STEP 3
Add a few splashes of vanilla extract.

STEP 4
Stir and enjoy!

7

2 how to say "I'M SORRY"

Oof! Apologizing to someone is never easy. But, it's super important. Whether you've ruined your brother's shirt or accidentally left your best friend out of plans, we all make mistakes. The best thing you can do is fess up and apologize.

Mean it.

People can feel your intentions. If you're saying "sorry" just to make someone happy, the person you're apologizing to can probably tell. So, before you say something, consider these questions:

Why are you really saying "sorry"?

Were your **actions** the best example of **who you are?**

Did you make someone **feel bad?**

Then, be honest and sincere when you say you're sorry.

Be specific.
Say exactly what it is you're sorry for and why.

Don't: I'm sorry about that thing I did, but I'm not sure why.

Do: I'm sorry for spilling spaghetti sauce on your shirt. It was an accident.

Don't make excuses.
The point of an apology is to own up to something you did. It's not the time to explain why it wasn't your fault.

Don't: I'm sorry for spilling spaghetti sauce on your shirt, but your shirt shouldn't have been so close to my plate.

Do: I'm sorry for spilling spaghetti sauce on your shirt. I should be more careful.

Offer a solution.
If there's a way you can make the situation a little better, or even do better in the future, say so.

Don't: I'm sorry for spilling spaghetti sauce on your shirt. Good luck with that.

Do: I'm sorry for spilling spaghetti sauce on your shirt. I'll wash it for you.

9

How to Fold ORIGAMI

(It's the perfect way to brighten someone's day!)

3

To get you started, here's how to fold an origami boat (that actually floats!).

Step 1.
Start with a rectangular piece of paper. Fold it left to right, then reopen it.

Step 2. Now fold it in half by bringing the top edge down to the bottom.

Step 3. Fold both the top left and right corners down toward the center of the rectangle.

Step 4. Fold each of the bottom, open edges upward.

Step 5. Now bring the two opposite, open corners toward each other and fold to form a square.

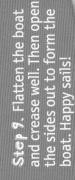

Step 6. Fold each of the open corners up toward its opposite corner, forming a triangle.

Step 7. Now, repeat the motion you made in Step 5. Push the two open corners of the triangle toward each other and fold, forming a square.

Step 8. Take each of the outer corners of the square and pull them away from each other to unfold the boat.

Step 9. Flatten the boat and crease well. Then open the sides out to form the boat. Happy sails!

4

How to help someone who's choking

If someone is really choking, he can't speak, breathe, or cough. Here's what you need to do right away:

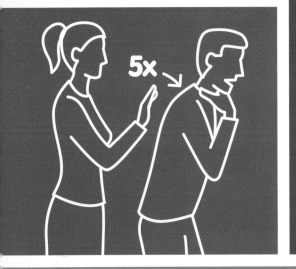

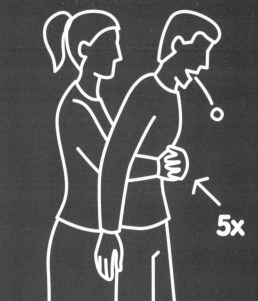

1. **Call 911,** or have someone else call.

2. Lean the person forward and give **five blows to the back.** Hit between the person's shoulder blades with the heel of your hand.

3. Give **five abdominal thrusts.** Wrap your arms around the person's waist. Make a fist with one hand. Place the thumb side of the fist just above the person's navel. Then grab your fist with the other hand and thrust up, with a hard, quick motion.

4. **Repeat back blows and abdominal thrusts** until the blockage comes out, and the person can breathe or cough.

If the person loses consciousness, gently help him to the floor, being careful of his head. If possible, clear the airway and begin CPR (cardiopulmonary resuscitation), but only if you've been trained how to do it.

The steps here are not the same ones you'd use for an infant. To learn more, sign up to take a first aid or CPR course at the American Red Cross by visiting www.redcross.org.

13

HOW TO

5

CONDUCT
AN EXPERIMENT

What's not to love about marshmallows?
They're **delicious,** they're **sweet,** and they're
super squishy. You can **stretch** them, **roast**
them, or put them in **hot chocolate.** But **what
would happen** if you left a marshmallow in
water for one week? What about soda?
Or vinegar?

To find out, you'll need to do what scientists do
to get answers to their questions—use the
scientific method. So break out the beakers,
unleash your inner Einstein, and turn the page
to get started!

THE **SCIENTIFIC** METHOD

STEP 1. **ASK A QUESTION.**
The question needs to be specific so that it can be tested and the results can be measured.

> EXAMPLE: Does the type of liquid affect how quickly a marshmallow dissolves?

STEP 2. **DO BACKGROUND RESEARCH.**
Find out as much as you can about the different parts of your experiment.

> EXAMPLE: What are marshmallows made of? What makes one liquid dissolve the marshmallow faster than another?

STEP 3. **CONSTRUCT A HYPOTHESIS.**
A hypothesis is an educated guess about what the results will be. So, now that you've done your research, you're qualified to hypothesize!

> EXAMPLE: Your hypothesis might be: I think that the type of liquid will affect how quickly a marshmallow dissolves. I think the marshmallow will dissolve slowest in water and fastest in soda.

STEP 4. **TEST YOUR HYPOTHESIS BY DOING AN EXPERIMENT.**
Now, put your hypothesis to the test by designing an experiment. The only variables that should change are the ones you're testing. Be sure to document your methods carefully, so that anyone could repeat your experiment.

> EXAMPLE: The marshmallows should be the same color and size, the liquid should be the same temperature, and the marshmallows should be left in the liquid the same amount of time. The only thing that will change is the type of liquid that the marshmallow is in.

STEP 5. **ANALYZE YOUR DATA AND DRAW A CONCLUSION.**
Make sure to keep careful notes and measurements as you conduct your test. When the experiment is complete, look over all of the information you've collected and answer your original question.

> EXAMPLE: Every day, look at your marshmallows and record your observations. Then, after a week, take the remaining marshmallows out of the liquid and measure them. Did the type of liquid affect how fast the marshmallows dissolved?

STEP 6. **REPORT YOUR RESULTS.**
Share your experiment and the discoveries that you made. You might write your findings up in a report, present them to your class, or put them on a snazzy display board for the science fair!

6

HOW TO HAVE

THICKER SKIN

Criticism of any kind can be really hard to hear. But it's important not to let what someone says about you make you feel bad about yourself.

🛈 Remember that almost all successful people have faced rejection, or been told they're not good enough, before they made it. Failing is a part of the path to success.

🛈 Give yourself time to be sad. Then, revisit the feedback you received. Could any of it help you improve? Try to use the criticism to improve upon a weak spot.

🛈 Have an uplifting statement to keep in mind when you start doubting yourself. For example, "I may feel down today, but I will start again tomorrow. I believe in myself, I believe in my abilities, and I won't give up on my goals!"

🛈 Dismiss the opinions of mean people. Only listen to the opinions of people you admire and trust, and who are trying to help you become better.

HOW TO MAKE

7

AN EDIBLE GIFT

Nathan Odom may be only 13 years old, but he's already achieved big-time success. Nathan won the third season of the kids' cooking competition show, *MasterChef Junior* on FOX. Here, he shares his recipe for **Double Chocolate Macarons**, which make a perfect tasty treat. If you're a baking newbie, start with a simple sugar cookie, then work your way up to this munchie masterpiece.

" Cookies are great for sharing with people," says Nathan. "And when someone knows that you worked hard to make food for them, it's more meaningful than something that's store-bought. **"**

DOUBLE CHOCOLATE MACARON

2 cups (256 g) powdered sugar
3/4 cup + 2 tablespoons (96 g) almond
flour

2 tablespoons (15 g) cocoa powder
4 egg whites
1/2 cup (100 g) granulated sugar

Preheat the oven to 350 degrees Fahrenheit (177°C).

Sift together the powdered sugar, almond flour, and cocoa powder. Discard anything that doesn't go through the sieve. (If the texture of this mixture is very gritty, grind for a few seconds in a food processor.)

In the bowl of a stand mixer, or by hand, whisk the egg whites until foamy, and add sugar in three additions, whisking between each. Whisk the egg mixture until a peak raises up that stays straight and doesn't curl when you lift the whisk.

Slowly fold the dry mixture into the meringue. Occasionally pat down the mixture in the bowl with your spoon or spatula, in order to push some air out of it.

When the mixture forms a slow, ribbon-like texture, and sinks back into the bowl after about 20 seconds, stop folding and pour into a piping bag.

On two lined sheet trays, pipe small circles, about an inch in diameter.

Once the mixture is gone, smack the sheet trays on the counter five times each.

Rest the macarons for 15 minutes.

Place the trays into the oven on the top rack, and bake for about 15 minutes, or until the macarons don't budge when given a light tap. If there isn't enough room in the oven for both sheets, bake them one at a time.

Set them aside to let them cool.

CHOCOLATE BUTTERCREAM

2 sticks unsalted room-temperature butter
6 egg yolks
2/3 cup (146 g) granulated sugar

1/3 cup and 5 teaspoons (310 mL) milk
1/4 cup (30 g) cocoa powder
1/2 teaspoon (2.5 mL) orange extract (optional)

Whisk together egg yolks and sugar until mixture is pale yellow and sugar is dissolved.

- -

Add milk and set aside.

- -

Mash butter with fork until no chunks remain.

- -

Pour egg mixture into a saucepan, and **heat on medium** heat, whisking continuously.

- -

When the egg mixture resembles custard, **pour it back into a large bowl** and whisk it until no longer hot.

- -

Add the butter and cocoa powder alternately in four batches, whisking between each addition. Add the orange extract, if using, and mix well. **Scrape into a piping bag** and pipe between two macaron shells.

- -

Yields about 12 macarons.

NATHAN'S FIVE FAVORITES

FAVORITE WAY TO CREATE NEW RECIPES: I find something that looks interesting to me in the pantry, and then I try to think of how I can elevate it and make it better.

FAVORITE KITCHEN TOOL: The stand mixer. It's very efficient for baking, and I'm really into baking.

FAVORITE COOKING CHALLENGE: Working with chocolate! It's incredibly difficult and is probably going to take me a while to master.

FAVORITE TAKEAWAY FROM *MASTERCHEF JUNIOR:* To think of crazy flavor combinations, and just try them. Even if they don't work, you've learned something for the future.

FAVORITE THING ABOUT COOKING: Cooking is a creative outlet and a way for me to express my emotions. If I'm not in a good mood, just thinking about cooking makes me really happy.

8 HOW TO PUMP GAS

(We know, we know, you can't even drive yet, but you'll be road-trippin' in no time.)

TIPS FOR BECOMING A GAS-PUMPING PRO

- Know which side of the car the gas tank is on.

- Make sure the car's engine is off before you begin pumping.

- Know which kind of gas the car takes, unleaded or diesel.

- After you've chosen the type of gas, there's often a lever on the pump that you need to lift, or a button you need to press, before you can begin pumping.

- Put the pump into the car first before squeezing the lever!

- Squeeze the lever inside the pump's handle until you've put as much gas in as you'd like. When the lever snaps back, your tank is full.

- After you've finished pumping your gas, put the gas cap back on right away. It's no fun (and not uncommon) to lose your gas cap after driving away with it still on the trunk or roof of your car.

THIS SALE $

GALLONS

Unleaded   Plus   Premium

87   89   91

weird but true!

CARS CAN BE MADE TO RUN ON ALL KINDS OF FUEL, INCLUDING COOKING OIL, GREASE, ETHANOL (MADE FROM CORN OR SUGARCANE), ELECTRICITY, OR EVEN COMPRESSED AIR.

25

How to WRITE a CHECK

(It's a dying art.)

9

Here you write the **date.**

In this box, you write the **check amount** in **numeral** form. For example: $20.25.

The **person or business's name** to whom you're writing the check goes here.

DOLLARS

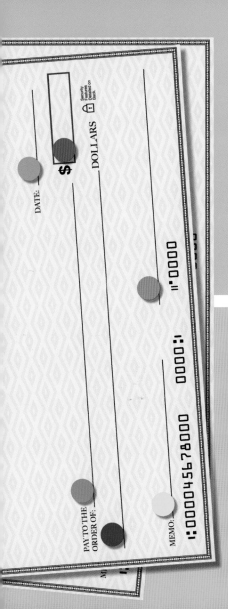

● On this line, you write out the check's **dollar amount.** Then, you write the **change** as a fraction of 100 (since there are 100 cents in one dollar). For example: $20.25 is written as "Twenty dollars and 25/100." Writing out the amount guarantees that no one can change the numbers you write in the box (or add more). Also, having the amount written two different ways is helpful if your handwriting isn't clear.

● The **memo line** is where you can write an **unofficial note** to yourself or to the recipient of the check. Since you're able to look at copies of your checks once they're cashed, you can write something such as "groceries" or "field trip" on this line to keep track of why you wrote the check.

● This is where you **sign your name,** to verify that you **authorize** the withdrawal from your bank account.

How to resolve  CONFLICT peacefully

TAKE A TIME-OUT. Conflicts can escalate when people say mean things because they are angry, hurt, or frustrated. So, stop, take a deep breath, and think before you say something you might regret later.

WATCH YOUR BODY LANGUAGE. Try not to scowl, cross your arms, or huff and puff.

SWALLOW YOUR PRIDE. Sometimes not wanting to admit you're wrong keeps you from saying "I'm sorry." But to become a better person, you have to acknowledge that you make mistakes, too.

LISTEN. If someone is mad at you, it's a natural reaction to want to defend yourself. But try to hear what the other person is saying and to understand how he is feeling.

SAYING "I." Instead of telling someone that what she did was wrong, explain how it made you feel. Try saying, "I feel _____ when you _____."

FORGIVE. This isn't easy, especially if someone has hurt your feelings. But it's important to remember that we all mess up.

NO NAME-CALLING. When you call someone names, the other person will likely get defensive. Not only is it mean, name-calling won't help you reach a resolution.

STEP AWAY. Sometimes the best thing to do is to leave for a bit, with the understanding that you'll talk more later. This can help you calm down and even see things from a different perspective.

HOW TO DO LAUNDRY

YOU DON'T WANT TO BE THE ONLY KID IN YOUR COLLEGE DORM SENDING YOUR DIRTY CLOTHES HOME TO MOM AND DAD!

Washing & Drying 101

👕 Wash dark and brightly colored clothes separately from light and white clothes.

👕 Check all pockets. Things like lip balm, gum, or candy can melt and stain your clothes. Also, you don't want to wash an important ticket or note or dollar bills!

👕 Don't put more soap in the washing machine than the directions call for. The bubbles can overflow and spill onto the floor. You may enjoy bubble surfing, but chances are your parents won't find it as fun.

👕 Rub stain remover or detergent directly on stains before washing.

👕 Read the tags in your clothes. Some clothes shouldn't be dried in the dryer, and others can only be washed by hand.

👕 Try to fold your laundry right after it is done drying. The longer clothes sit in a dryer or laundry basket, the more wrinkled they will be.

👕 Clean the lint out of the lint basket after you use the dryer.

12
How to say "No"

Nobody *loves* turning people down, but it's important to resist the urge to say "yes" to things you don't really want to do just to please someone.

Don't offer too much **EXPLANATION** as to **WHY** you're saying "no." The more **EXCUSES** you give, the more someone might try to **NEGOTIATE** with you.

Think of a way to **EXPRESS** yourself **HONESTLY** while still being true to **WHO YOU ARE**. Saying "no" doesn't mean you have to be **RUDE**. You can always say "Thanks for asking me, though," or **"MAYBE ANOTHER TIME."**

Keep your "no" **CLEAR, DIRECT, SHORT,** and **SIMPLE.** For example, you can say, "I can't this week." Or "Sorry, I'm pretty busy right now—I have other commitments."

How to tie

three basic

KNOTS

Sure, you can knot a string and tie your shoes—but what about when you're an adult and have to do adult things ... like tie furniture to the roof of a car or survive on a desert island?

BOWLINE

A secure loop at the end of a line that is always easy to untie

Step 1

Create a small loop in the rope.

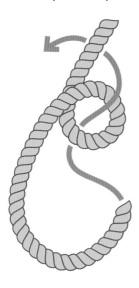

Step 2

Weave the end of the rope up through the loop, then back around the straight, top part of the rope …

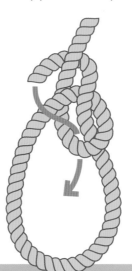

Step 3

… and back down through the small loop.

SQUARE KNOT

This knot is used to tie a rope around a structure, like the sail of a boat.

Place the ends of two separate ropes side by side. Wrap the right rope over, then under the left rope, and then pull it upward. The ends of both ropes should be facing up.

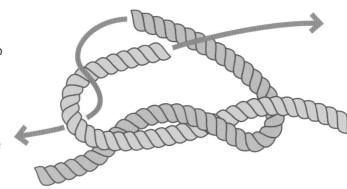

Now take the rope end on the left (which is actually the right rope) and weave it over, then under the rope end on the right. Pull to tighten.

SHEET BEND

This knot is used to tie two different ropes together.

Step 1

Fold the end of rope 1 up alongside itself (forming a U where the sides are touching). Then take rope 2, pass it under and through the middle of the U shape in rope 1, then behind both the shorter end of rope 1 and the longer end of rope 1 (in that order) ...

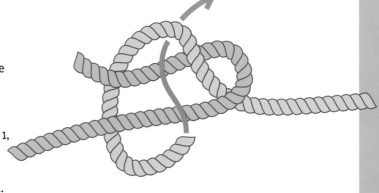

Step 2

... then underneath itself, rope 2. Pull to tighten.

HOW TO WRITE A GREAT
THANK-YOU NOTE

14

When someone does something nice that makes you happy, it's really important to say "Thank you." The best way is to send a note that expresses your gratitude. It's a surefire way to make the person feel great, and there's a bonus—you'll feel great, too!

Here's how to write an A+ thank-you note:

▶ **GET CREATIVE WITH YOUR CARD.** Pick stationery that appeals to you, or—better yet—make something!

CONSTRUCTING YOUR CARD:

1 Find a piece of poster board, construction paper, or any other piece of thick paper.

2 Cut a small rectangle, about 4 inches x 5 inches (10 cm x 12.5 cm).

3 Fold it in half.

4 Decorate the front with markers, glitter, stamps, leaves, flowers, or anything else you like.

You'll need:

THINGS TO WRITE
AND DOODLE WITH

PAPER

SCISSORS

▶ **BE POLITE.** Begin your note with a formal greeting, such as "Dear Gail," and end it with a warm sign-off such as "Many thanks."

▶ **WRITE NEATLY.** You don't want to send a card that no one can read.

▶ **BE SPECIFIC.** State exactly what you're thanking the person for.

▶ **GET PERSONAL.** Explain how you plan to use the gift or what their gesture meant to you.

15 How to figure something out on your own

So, you want to learn how to do something you've never done before? Your first thought might be to ask an adult for help, which is fine. But why not give it a go on your own first? You can learn a lot by doing something by yourself. It can be frustrating at first, but tinkering around and sticking with it until you find a solution leads to independence (and less parental nagging!).

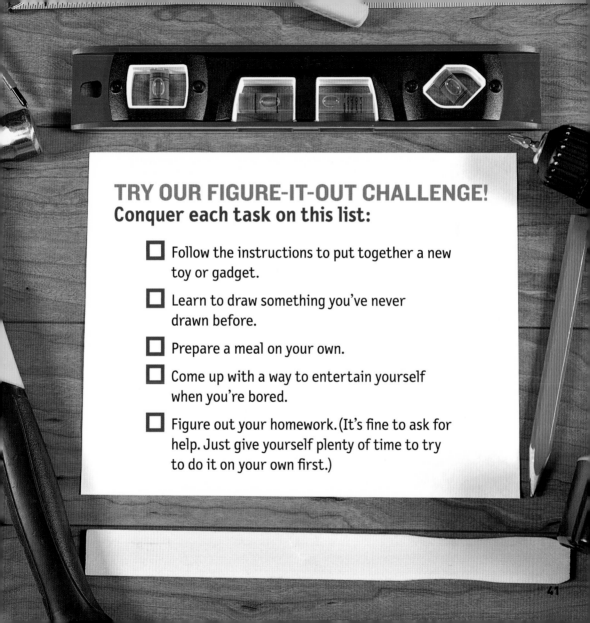

TRY OUR FIGURE-IT-OUT CHALLENGE!
Conquer each task on this list:

☐ Follow the instructions to put together a new toy or gadget.

☐ Learn to draw something you've never drawn before.

☐ Prepare a meal on your own.

☐ Come up with a way to entertain yourself when you're bored.

☐ Figure out your homework. (It's fine to ask for help. Just give yourself plenty of time to try to do it on your own first.)

16 How to ask for help

Just like it's important to figure out some things on your own, it's also important to know when and how to ask for help. **Think about asking for help when:**

- You haven't been able to find a solution to a problem, and you don't know what else to try.
- There are skills you'd like to learn, but you need to be taught first.
- There will be serious or negative consequences if you don't solve the problem.
- You feel worried or concerned about a particular problem or situation.

Also, if you're not sure if you should ask for help or try to work it out on your own, run it by a trusted adult. You can say, "I want to be independent and try to problem-solve on my own, but what do you think about this situation?"

Remember: Always ask for help if you're scared, in danger, if there are serious consequences to your problem, or you're feeling helpless or hopeless. And, if the first person you ask isn't able to help, ask someone else. Keep asking people until you find the help you need.

17

HOW TO
BUILD
A CAMP-
FIRE

(AND HOW TO PUT ONE OUT)

DON'T FORGET THE S'MORES!

What You'll Need:

TINDER
This is usually small, very dry sticks, bark, paper, and/or branches used to start the fire. If you're using paper or newspaper, twist it tightly so that it resembles a twig. If the paper is long enough, after you twist it, tie it into a knot. It will burn better that way.

KINDLING
This is what really gets the fire going. You'll need dry wood that is bigger than the wood used for tinder, but still less than one inch (2.5 cm) thick.

LOGS
These are the fuel that will keep your fire burning. Logs should be dry and one to five inches (2.5 to 12.5 cm) thick.

MATCHES
To light the tinder to start your fire.

WATER
To put your fire out.

A SAFE SPACE
A structured fire pit at least ten feet (3 m) from trees, bushes, or anything that could catch fire, in a place that permits campfires. If there is not a ring of large rocks around the pit, create one.

How to Build a Campfire:

STEP 1: Put a pile of tinder in the middle of the fire pit.

STEP 2: Stack the kindling on top of the tinder in a loose teepee formation. Leave open spaces between the kindling. (It's important that air be able to flow through the structure. Fire needs air to burn.)

STEP 3: Around the kindling teepee, create a teepee with your fuel logs.

STEP 4: Light the tinder with a match. The tinder should light the kindling, which eventually should light the logs.

STEP 5: When the teepee falls, add a few more fuel logs to the fire to keep it going.

How to **Put Out** a Campfire:

STEP 1: Let all of the wood burn completely so that only ash remains. (Never, ever go to sleep while the fire still has embers.)

STEP 2: Sprinkle water over the fire until there is no steam rising and there are no more hissing sounds.

STEP 3: Use a stick to move the logs and ash around to make sure there are no remaining live embers.

STEP 4: When you're sure the fire is completely out, sprinkle more water over it, to be safe.

STEP 5: Check the ground around the fire pit to be sure that no live sparks or embers flew out onto the surrounding area.

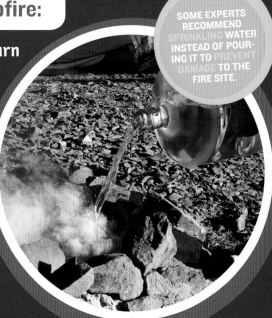

SOME EXPERTS RECOMMEND SPRINKLING WATER INSTEAD OF POURING IT TO PREVENT DAMAGE TO THE FIRE SITE.

HOW TO journal LIKE A PRO

This isn't so much a **"how you should,"** as it's a "how you **could."** That's because your journal is **your own**— your own **style,** your own **sensibilities,** your own **voice.**

18

There are **dozens** of **different ways** to do it:

Some people write in their journals like they're corresponding with a pen pal, while other people write everything they did that day. Some people write about their feelings, hopes, and dreams. Other people **make lists, write poems, or draw pictures.** Your journal is completely up to you. Just don't forget to have fun!

19

How to go after something with

Meet
National Geographic
Emerging Explorer

NATALIA LEDFORD

Natalia is a documentary filmmaker, storyteller, and social entrepreneur. She started shooting her first documentary when she was just a junior in high school. The film was about a group of her classmates who moved to the United States to flee the civil war in Sudan. Natalia, who continues to make documentaries, now lives in Guatemala. She started a project there for women in need, to sell their crafts and jewelry.

Natalia's Tips for Discovering Your Passion and Going For It:

1 Think about what you loved when you were younger. Storytelling has been something I've done since I was a small child. Then, in elementary school, I started filling notebooks with stories.

2 Have fun. When I was 14, I used to make goofy videos with my friend for fun. Looking back, I realize that was how I learned to use cameras and editing software. If you love what you do, learning the necessary skills will come naturally.

3 Set a goal. Then, make a list of all the skills you need to learn, and the steps you need to take, to achieve it.

4 Use your passion to do good. When you discover what it is you love to do, find a way to apply it to a job that helps other people or the planet.

5 Be open to new paths. I never would have thought that I'd be learning about business. But now I am, so I can manage a project that supports women entrepreneurs in Guatemala. Remember, you're never too old, or too young, to learn something new.

HOW TO START A
PETITION

IS THERE SOMETHING YOU'D LIKE TO SEE CHANGE?

Do other people feel the same way? One way to show leaders how many people care about a particular issue is by starting a petition. A petition is a request to a person in charge with a **LIST OF SIGNATURES** from people who support that change. The request could be that the cafeteria stop serving mystery meat or that lights be installed at the local skate park. You could even petition your parents to stop letting Uncle Bob choose the movie for family movie night!

You can start a petition by writing your request on a piece of paper and asking people to sign it, or you can create one online on websites like Change.org.

21

How to Balance a Spoon on Your Nose

Why is this one of 100 things you should know before you grow up? Because sometimes you need to **stop being serious** and be **silly** for a second. So, push those **table manners** aside and show off your **secret skills!**

· ·

STEP 1
Wipe off your nose and a spoon with a napkin or tissue.

STEP 2
Breathe onto the inside of the spoon.

STEP 3
Hang the spoon from the tip of your nose.

weird but true!
THE GUINNESS WORLD RECORD FOR NUMBER OF SPOONS BALANCED ON SOMEONE'S FACE IS 31!

STEP 4
See how long you can keep it perched there, or have a contest with your friends to see who can do it the longest!

How to Make

22

a Cool Craft

How to tie-dye a T-shirt

Step 1: Set up a workspace outside using trash bags or a plastic tarp to cover your work area. Tie-dying is very fun, but very messy. The dye will stain anything it touches, so use disposable rubber gloves, and have lots of rags or paper towels handy.

Step 2: Lay flat the shirt that you're going to dye. Then, roll it up for stripes or pinch from the middle for circles. Next, secure 3 to 12 rubber bands around the shirt. The more bands you use, the more stripes you'll have.

Step 3: Next, put the different color dyes in separate bowls or squirt bottles. Now, get creative! Either dip your shirt or squirt the dye onto it. Use as many colors as you want!

Step 4: Wrap the shirt in a plastic bag and let the dye set for six to eight hours.

Step 5: Take the shirt out of the plastic bag (wear gloves to avoid dyed fingers!). Then, take the rubber bands off and rinse the shirt in cold water to get rid of excess dye.

Step 6: Wash your shirt in the washing machine by itself, so that it doesn't dye any other clothes. Then, put the shirt in the dryer by itself or hang it up to dry.

Step 7: Wear your new shirt proudly, and show off your handiwork to your friends!

How to
make your bed
(and score major brownie points with your parents!)

23

It might sound like **one more thing** to check off your **chore chart**, but making your bed is actually a great way to get your day started **on the right foot**—not to mention, it's an easy way to make your room look a lot more **put together**, pronto.

And while there's **no right or wrong way to do it**, here are some **hints** for how to make your nest neat.

Step 1: Remove all sneakers, devices, and half-eaten sandwiches from your bed.

Step 2: Pull the bottom sheet tight to remove wrinkles and tuck it around the sides and underneath your mattress.

Step 3: Then place your nonfitted sheet, or flat sheet, on top. Leave it flat or fold it back—that's up to you.

Step 4: Top it off with your comforter, quilt, or blanket. Then smooth the covers to create a polished look. Fluff your pillows and arrange them neatly at the head of your bed.

Step 5: Resist the urge to put the items you removed during Step 1 back onto your neatly made bed—that would totally undo all your efforts. Now, step back, admire your work, and go rule the rest of your day!

24 How to deal with CHANGE

Change can be hard. It's normal to want things to stay the same. But some of the coolest things that will happen in your life will happen after some sort of change. Change is something you can't avoid. So it's important that you find ways to make it a little less uncomfortable.

1 **It's okay to be sad.** Maybe you've moved to a new city, or you're going to a new school. It's natural to be sad to leave friends and situations that were comfortable.

2 **Give it time.** Remember that even if you're not loving this new change now, that doesn't mean you'll feel this way forever. It takes time to adjust and get used to new situations.

3 Find something that's familiar. Even in a new environment, you can find things that feel familiar. If you move to a new home, consider setting up your room similar to the way you had it in your old home.

4 Develop routines. Routines help us feel comfortable. Try establishing an after-school ritual that you enjoy, or maybe your family decides that every Friday, you'll order pizza and watch a movie.

5 Celebrate small victories. Did you find a delicious gluten-free cookie recipe after you could no longer eat gluten? Make sure to notice anything good that happens after a change.

HOW TO
RAISE MONEY
FOR A GOOD CAUSE

If only money did grow on trees, it'd be a lot easier to find when you needed some. But, for now, if your class wants to go on a cool trip, or you're raising money for a local charity, you'll need to **find creative ways to make some moolah.** Gather some friends, ask an adult to help supervise, and brainstorm. **Make signs** to advertise your efforts, and be sure to include what you're raising money for. People will be more likely to help if they **know** their **money** is **going** to a **good cause.**

HERE ARE SOME IDEAS TO GET YOU STARTED >>>>

> **Start a leaf-raking or weed-pulling service**

> Have a yard sale

25

Water neighbors' plants while they're away

> Help with odd jobs, like washing windows or painting a fence

> Pet sit for your neighbors

26 HOW to be Worldly

Did you know that the number one way people get around in **THE NETHERLANDS** is by bicycle? In fact, there are more bicycles there than people! And in **INDIA,** there is a school with more than **45,000** students ages 3 to 17. It's the **BIGGEST** school in the **WORLD!**

Being worldly means being interested in what's going on beyond your neighborhood, your town, or your country. Even if you can't hop on a plane to TOKYO tomorrow, there are still lots of things you can do to LEARN about other PEOPLE, COUNTRIES, and CULTURES. For starters, ask questions, be a GOOD LISTENER, and be open to NEW IDEAS.

➡ READ the newspaper, watch the news, or listen to news radio.

➡ WATCH a foreign film.

➡ EXPLORE somewhere new—even if it's just the next town over!

➡ LEARN another language.

TRY food from another country.

LEARN more about world history.

FIND the places in the news on a map.

BE OPEN to new information, experiences, or relationships that challenge your old opinions.

27 HOW TO BE
DISCIPLINED

(and become a goal-reaching, dream-achieving superstar!)

NO, we're not talking about your parents grounding you for not finishing your chores. This type of discipline means doing what you've made up your mind to do, even when you don't feel like it. Things like practicing piano when you'd rather be watching TV, or being nice to your little brother even when he's annoying you.

HERE ARE SOME WAYS TO AMP UP YOUR "STICK-TO-IT-IVE-NESS."

TREAT YOUR GOAL LIKE A PUPPY.
Give it a name (be clear and specific about what your goal is), tell your friends and family about it (their support will motivate you!), and protect it (stay away from things that might distract you or keep you from achieving it).

JUST DO IT. If you wait until you feel like doing something, you may never do it (ahem, homework).

COMPLETE THE MISSION. Get in the habit of doing what you say you're going to do and finishing what you start.

DON'T GIVE UP. Stick with your plan, even if you mess up. Just start again the next day. People who are disciplined aren't perfect—they just don't give up.

HOW TO
HANDLE AN
EMERGENCY

28

Think fast! There's smoke in your kitchen, there's severe weather in your area, or your best friend falls off her bike! Being prepared for an emergency situation means having a plan for how you'll react when one happens.

Dr. Andrew MacPherson is an emergency and trauma physician, a member of the Red Cross, and on the ski patrol at Whistler Blackcomb Mountains in Victoria, British Columbia, Canada. If anyone knows how to handle himself in an emergency, it's him. From the emergency room to the side of a mountain, he has to be prepared to do first aid just about anywhere. "It's pretty cool," Dr. MacPherson said. "You really have to think on your feet."

Check out this Q&A to learn HOW and WHY you should be an emergency preparedness pro!

Q: What are some of the emergency situations people should prepare for, and how should they prepare?

A: CPR (cardiopulmonary resuscitation) and first aid training are important. One in four people will be in a situation in which someone may need CPR. First aid training is important in order to know how to respond to common household emergencies like burns, cuts, sprains, and falls. Sign up at a local community center or hospital.

You should also be prepared for natural disasters, such as hurricanes and tornadoes, as well as house fires.

> **MAKE A FAMILY FIRE PLAN!**
> You should know how to get out of the house, where you'll meet, and which neighbor's house you'll go to. Also make sure you have smoke detectors that are working properly. Remind your parents to test them once a month and replace the batteries at least once a year.

Q: What's the best way someone can respond to an emergency?

A: It's very important to try to **stay calm.** One way to do that is by learning what to do before something happens.

Then stop and take stock of the situation. If you need to, **call 911,** or send someone else to call 911 so that you can stay with the injured.

Assess the situation **based on your training,** and take your time.

Be polite and professional, and know when it's time to let someone with more training take over.

MAKE YOUR OWN
FIRST AID KIT

Dr. MacPherson's Medical Must-Have's

1. A book or a guide that explains how to respond to different injuries, if you don't administer first aid on a regular basis

2. Nitrile gloves, since some people are allergic to latex gloves

3. Bandages (in assorted sizes), sterile gauze, adhesive tape, and antibiotic ointment for wounds

4. Tweezers to remove splinters and ticks

5. Cold compresses for injuries that are swelling

6. Scissors to cut off clothes if you need to

7. An emergency blanket or some sort of warm weather protective gear, depending on where you live

The Red Cross now has an app you can download that details how to respond to various emergencies.

HOW TO
PLANT
SOMETHING
(AND KEEP IT ALIVE)

Dying for a dog, but Mom won't let you have one? Show off your nurturing know-how by taking care of something a bit simpler first.

Every species of plant requires **different care** to grow and thrive. Some need direct light, while some need shade. Some need watering every day. Others can go without water for weeks! To give your plant pal the best shot, find out exactly **what conditions it prefers.** Be sure to consider what kind of **fertilizer** it should get, how much **space** it needs to grow, the best **temperature** for the plant, and the type of **soil** it requires.

Or, if you're feeling adventurous, **buy a seed "grab bag,"** which has an assortment of different seeds to plant. Then, in a few weeks, you'll be surprised by what sprouts.

how to
EDIT a VIDEO

30

NOWADAYS, YOU DON'T HAVE TO BE STEVEN SPIELBERG TO DIRECT A GREAT FILM. With just a digital camera, or even a smartphone, anyone can be a filmmaker. To learn how to edit your videos, take a class, read a book on the subject, or check out one of the many tutorials online. Aaaannd action!

BEFORE FILMS HAD SOUND, SOMETIMES ACTORS WOULD PERFORM DIALOGUE LIVE IN THE THEATER AS THE SILENT FILM WAS PROJECTED ON A SCREEN.

31

HOW TO BE
BRAVE

Everyone feels afraid from time to time, but it's how you respond to that fear that shows you who you are. Being scared is an uncomfortable feeling, so it makes sense that you'd want to avoid it. But the only way to conquer a fear is to do the thing that scares you. As Mark Twain said, "Courage is resistance to fear, mastery of fear, not absence of fear."

MALALA YOUSAFZAI

Malala is the **youngest person to have ever won a Nobel Peace Prize.** She won it in 2014, when she was just 17 years old. Malala was born in Pakistan in 1997. She attended a school founded by her father and quickly became an advocate for **a girl's right to get an education.** However, the Taliban, a violent political group in her country, believed that girls should not go to school.

Malala spoke out against the Taliban in favor of education for girls and soon became a target of the Taliban. She didn't believe they would harm her, because she was just a young girl. But in 2012, on her way home from school, a member of the Taliban **shot her.** One of the bullets hit her on the left side of her face. She survived the attack, which also injured two of her friends. She was eventually sent to a hospital in England to receive treatment.

What she went through was enough to make even the strongest person hide in fear. But Malala did not. She believes too strongly in her message, and so she **continues to speak out** about the importance of education and equality for women. She now attends school in England, and she wrote a book, *I Am Malala: The Girl Who Stood Up for Education and Was Shot by the Taliban.* On her 16th birthday, Malala gave a beautiful, powerful speech to the United Nations. In it, she said:

> **"They thought that the bullets would silence us, but they failed. And out of that silence came thousands of voices. The terrorists thought they would change my aims and stop my ambitions. But nothing changed in my life except this: weakness, fear, and hopelessness died. Strength, power, and courage was born."**

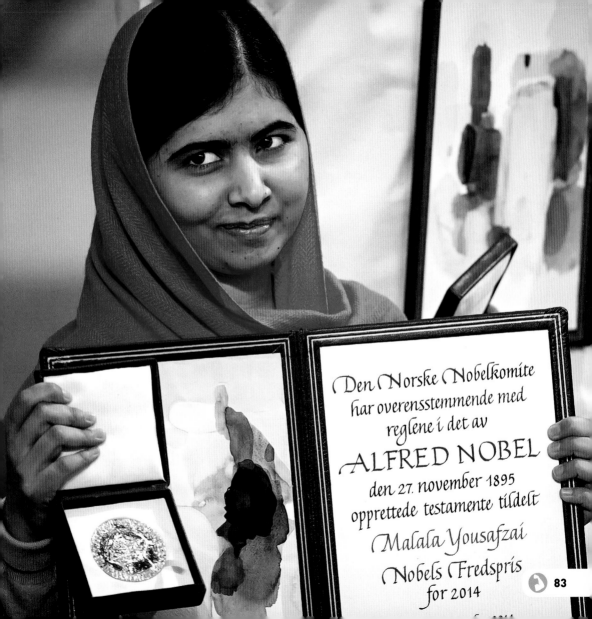

Den Norske Nobelkomite
har overensstemmende med
reglene i det av
ALFRED NOBEL
den 27. november 1895
opprettede testamente tildelt
Malala Yousafzai
Nobels Fredspris
for 2014

32

How to EXPRESS yourself

Have you ever opened a soda bottle after shaking it, and the soda exploded, spraying everywhere? That's kind of what happens if you bottle up your feelings. So, go ahead, get them out of your system.

It's best to express your feelings in little bits at a time, so that they don't all come rushing out at once. Emotions—like **anger, sadness, frustration,** and **excitement**—need to flow through you. When you hold your feelings in, or try to pretend they're not there, they can actually do **damage** to your **physical** and **mental health.**

The first step is to try to figure out what you're feeling and why. Are you **jealous? Hurt? Lonely?** Try to get to the root of where these feelings are coming from. Then **talk** to someone about how you feel. Or, if you don't feel like talking about it, **try one of these techniques:**

- **Find a song** that relates to how you feel. Turn it up loud and dance the emotion out.

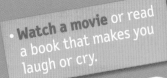
- **Watch a movie** or read a book that makes you laugh or cry.

- **Make a collage** of pictures that expresses the way you feel.

- **Meditate** or try a relaxation technique mentioned on page 228.

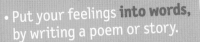
- Put your feelings **into words,** by writing a poem or story.

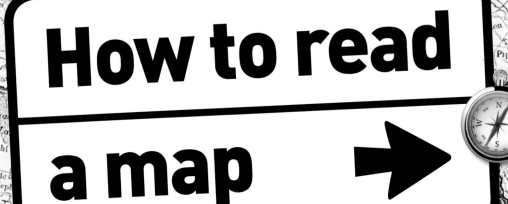

How to read a map

In the era of the smartphone, reading a map is becoming a lost art. But if you learn how to do it, you won't ever have to worry about getting lost!

➤ First, get familiar with the cardinal directions: north, south, east, and west.

➤ A map's scale tells you how to convert the units of measure on the map (like inches or centimeters) into units of measure on land (like miles or kilometers).

➤ A map's key will tell you what the symbols on the map represent. For example, red lines might be borders around states, a star might show the location of a state's capital, blue areas might represent a body of water, and a green line might be an interstate highway.

33

How to take care of your TEETH

It might seem **tedious now**, but you'll **thank** your younger **self** when you're **90** and still have a full **set of choppers!**

Brush your teeth **twice a day,** for at least two minutes each time.

Use a toothpaste that contains **fluoride.**

Floss between your teeth every day.

Avoid sugary snacks and drinks.

Don't **smoke!**

Visit your **dentist** regularly.

Eat **healthy foods.**

HOW TO BE
TRULY
GRATEFUL

35

If, every day, you **appreciate** what you have (instead of dwelling on what you don't have), you'll begin to notice you feel happier. Practicing **gratitude,** or thinking about all of the people and things you're **thankful** for, shifts your perspective. And it will change your life for the better.

36 How to keep your balance

If you've ever tried pulling on a shoe while standing on one foot, you know how important balance is. Your brain controls your sense of balance based on signals it receives from your eyes, inner ear, and other parts of your body like your skin and muscles. And, just like running or swimming, balance is something you can improve upon with practice.

Here are ten activities to help you work through your wobbles.

1. Ice-skating
2. Biking
3. Snowboarding
4. Yoga poses, like the side plank or half moon
5. Walking on a balance beam
6. Standing on one foot
7. Rollerblading
8. Riding a skateboard
9. Playing hopscotch
10. Riding a scooter

HOW TO RECOVER FROM embarrassment LIKE A Champ!

37

Getting embarrassed is no fun. Your heart starts beating faster, your stomach churns, and you might feel like crying. Even worse, it feels as if the whole world is laughing at you. But guess what? It happens to EVERYONE. And usually, people forget about it in a day, an hour, or even a few minutes.

So, the next time you slip on a banana peel and turn red as a tomato, try one of these tried-and-true recovery tactics and remember that this, too, shall pass:

- **LAUGH.** If you did something funny, such as walking around with toilet paper on your shoe or tripping on the sidewalk, instead of feeling bad about it—laugh.

- **BREATHE.** Take slow, deep breaths. It will help slow your heart rate and give you a moment to regroup.

- **ADDRESS IT.** Just like the bogeyman in your closet that turns out to be a pile of clothes, things are less scary if you shine a light on them. So, instead of pretending nothing happened, you could say, "Whoa, did you see that?" or "Wow, that was embarrassing."

- **TALK ABOUT SOMETHING ELSE.** Feelings are your body's way of reacting to your thoughts. So, think about something else. Try changing the topic of conversation. Talk about a new movie coming out, a test you're studying for, or someone's new puppy.

- **DOWNPLAY IT.** Tomorrow you won't even be thinking about it anymore. So, instead of making it a big deal, try this: shrug, smile, and say, "Oh, well."

38

HOW TO DO A CARD TRICK

STEP RIGHT UP!

COME ONE, COME ALL TO WITNESS THE AMAZING (INSERT YOUR NAME HERE)!

HERE'S ONE TO GET YOU STARTED:

1 Have your friend or a spectator shuffle your deck of cards. Tell him he can shuffle it as much as he likes. You want him to be sure there's nothing funny about the deck.

2 Fan out the deck and ask him to pick a card.

3 Tell him not to show it to you, but to look at the card and remember what it is.

4 Then, put the deck of cards face down in your left hand and split the deck with your right hand.

5 Tell the person to put the card face down on the cards in your left hand. At the same time, discreetly sneak a peek of the card that's face up in your right hand. Remember that card.

6 Put the cards in your right hand on top of the cards in your left.

7 Begin flipping the cards over on the table in front of you. When you get to the card you saw in your right hand earlier, the next card will be the card your friend chose. When you flip it over, pause a moment, as if you're getting a feeling and say "This is your card!"

HOW TO IDENTIFY AT LEAST ONE PLANET

39 WHEN **KNICOLE COLÓN**, AN ASTRONOMER AND NATIONAL GEOGRAPHIC YOUNG EXPLORER, WAS A YOUNG GIRL, her father would get the family up in the middle of the night to watch meteor showers. "We'd complain because it was early," said Knicole, "but it was always awesome to go in the backyard and see science happening." Then Knicole saw a couple of movies about space and aliens, which sparked her interest in the possibility of life on other planets. It was then, at the age of 12, that Knicole decided that she wanted to be an astronomer.

Q: WHAT DO YOU DO?

A: I study planets around other stars. We have discovered well over a thousand planets, which is a nice complement to the eight planets (and five dwarf planets) in our solar system.

Q: HOW DO YOU DISCOVER NEW PLANETS?

A: There are different techniques, but we take a bunch of images of one star, in a single night, to measure its brightness. If the brightness of that star dims by a small amount, and only for a few hours, that could mean a planet has passed in front of it and blocked some of its light. So, by measuring the dip in the star's brightness, we can tell the size of the planet that blocked the light.

Q: DO YOU GO OUT AT NIGHT TO TAKE PICTURES OF THE STARS?

A: Actually, now we have access to robotic telescopes. So I can do everything online. If I want to observe a certain star, I just enter the coordinates. The telescope will take the data and upload it to an archive. Then, the next day, I download it and analyze it. So now, I don't even need to be up every night observing.

Q: WHAT EXCITES YOU MOST ABOUT ASTRONOMY?

A: I love that astronomy is basically the oldest science. People studied astronomy thousands of years ago. We have records that people used from 1400 B.C. It's amazing! And, I love that we're still learning today. There's still so much that we don't know.

NOW IT'S YOUR TURN! *Expert Tip:* For the best visibility, go somewhere dark on a clear night, away from brightly lit areas.

KNICOLE'S PICKS FOR 3 MUST-SEE PLANETS

The first step to identifying a planet is to find the "ecliptic." The ecliptic is the path that the sun and the planets follow, as we see it from Earth. So, trace the path of the sun across the sky through the day. Then, at night, look along the same path to find planets in our solar system.

And, remember: The solar system planets are distinctive from stars because they don't "twinkle" like stars do.

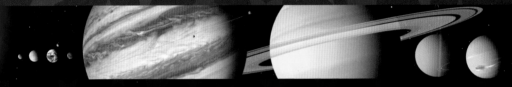

VENUS

Venus is often referred to as the "morning star" or "evening star," because it can only be seen close to the horizon within a few hours of sunrise or sunset, depending on the time of year. After the moon, it is the brightest object in the night sky and so is easy to pick out.

MARS

If you can find Venus in the night sky, then you can follow its path on the ecliptic (or just recall the sun's path in the daytime sky) to find other planets. Mars can be quite dim, but it has a distinct reddish color.

JUPITER

Jupiter is the third brightest object in the night sky (after Venus and the moon), and it appears bright white in color.

40

HOW *to* COME UP WITH THE PERFECT *secret* HANDSHAKE

This takes **practice** and a partner who's up to the **challenge**. But with some **imagination**, behind-the-back **hand claps**, and a few signature **dance moves**, you'll have a secret handshake you just may want to **share**.

How to turn an idea into reality

41

One day when **Arjun Kumar** was **12 years old,** he was very late getting home from school. His school bus had encountered heavy rain. When he arrived at his home in Chennai, Tamil Nadu in India, he found his parents had been very worried. Then, he had an idea: **What if there was an app** that **tracked school buses** so that parents could see exactly where their children were on their routes to and from school?

Luckily, technology had long been a passion of Arjun's. "I started using computers when I was two and a half years old," he says. "I remember playing with basic simulation software with a pile of pillows stacked on the chair so that I could reach the keyboard."

So, Arjun got to work and created that very app, which he named **Ez School Bus Locator.** He even won first place in the Kindergarten–8th grade category, in **MIT's App Inventor Contest** in 2012.

Here, Arjun, now 14 years old, shares what he's learned on his journey from tech-loving toddler to **CEO and app inventor!**

Start by identifying a problem. My motivation to create something new comes from the desire to help people around me. So, look for problems, and get inspiration from them.

Learn the new skills you'll need. Ez School Bus Locator was the very first app I had created, and I was new to developing apps using the Android system. So, the next step was to learn the new languages and the tools. When I'm learning something new, I mostly use trial and error and refer to resources on the Web. I try to figure out things myself, and ask for help from others only when absolutely necessary.

Brainstorm possible solutions. When I had the idea for Ez School Bus Locator, I spent many days brainstorming by myself and with my parents. I tried to keep the user in my mind when thinking about the app's design.

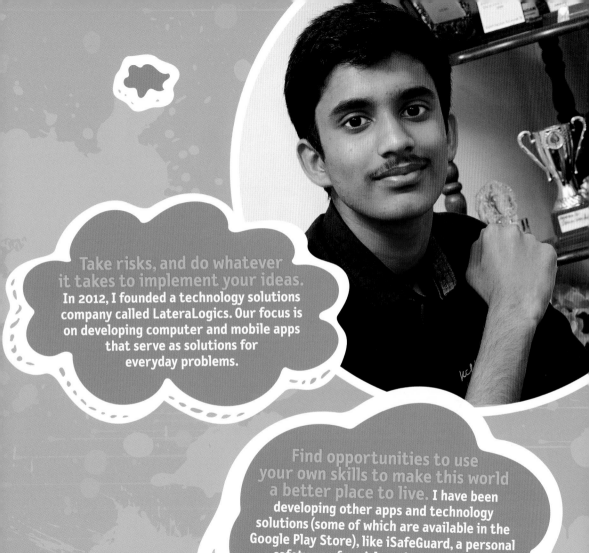

Take risks, and do whatever it takes to implement your ideas. In 2012, I founded a technology solutions company called LateraLogics. Our focus is on developing computer and mobile apps that serve as solutions for everyday problems.

Find opportunities to use your own skills to make this world a better place to live. I have been developing other apps and technology solutions (some of which are available in the Google Play Store), like iSafeGuard, a personal safety app for girls and young women.

How to remember someone's name

You know that awkward moment when you meet someone for the third time and *still* don't know the person's name? Here are some tips to make sure that doesn't happen again.

HELLO

my name is

Repeat it. When you meet someone, try to use his or her name right away. *For example: What about you, Abby, do you play any sports?*

Think of an image. Does the person's name sound at all like the name of an object you can remember? *For example: If someone's name is Sally, picture a sailboat. Then, the next time you see her, you might remember the picture of the sailboat first, and then that her name is Sally.*

Think about how it sounds. After you learn someone's name, say it in your head several times, exaggerating the syllables. *For example, if you meet someone named "Andy," think: Annnnnnn Deeeeeeee.*

Write it down. Writing things down can help commit them to memory. After you meet someone, jot his or her name down in a notebook or journal.

How to plan a PARTY

43

GUEST LIST:
Is it just a few close friends or a 50-person bash?

INVITATIONS:
Do you want to mail out paper invites or send electronically?

MENU:
The drinks, the food, and the cake!

MUSIC:
Pick the perfect tunes for the kind of vibe you want—do you want people to get down on the dance floor or maybe just mingle?

LOCATION:
At your home? In a gym? At a restaurant?

WHETHER OR NOT YOU WANT TO HAVE A THEME:
Are you throwing a formal tea party, or is it a dress-as-your-favorite-comic-book-character kind of shindig?

THE DAY AND TIME:
Think about how long you want your guests to stay.

GAMES OR ACTIVITIES:
What will you and your guests do to pass the time?

 111

How to **pack** a suitcase like a pro

44

No one wants to have the suitcase on the baggage carousel with underwear hanging out of it. Nor do you want to waste a single second—when you could be swimming in the pool!—searching for your bathing suit. That's why you need to be organized. "Being organized will save you time and aggravation," says the professional organizer himself, **Barry Izsak.**

Here, Barry shares 10 tips for a perfectly packed bag.

1 A few days before your trip, find out what the weather will be like where you're traveling. This will help you decide what clothes to bring.

2 Then, begin planning your outfits. To cut down on the amount of clothes you pack, bring items that you can wear more than once—like jeans, dark colors, or patterned pieces. White or light-colored clothes are more likely to show dirt or stains.

3 If you're traveling by plane, pack anything you might want during the flight in the bag that you'll keep under the seat (like snacks, books, electronics, disinfectant wipes, and any toiletries or medicine you'll need should your bag get lost).

4 The hanging toiletry bags that have multiple compartments are great for keeping your stuff organized. The clear pockets make it easy to see and find things.

5 Don't just throw everything into your suitcase. Keep your pants in one place in the bag, your socks in another, and so on. Then you know exactly where to look when you need something.

6 If you're going to arrive at your destination late, make sure whatever you're going to need right away (like your pajamas or toothbrush!) is at the top of your suitcase. Then you won't have to dig through all your clothes to find them.

7 Because shoes are so bulky, pick just two or three pairs to bring. Only pack outfits that will go with those.

8 If you know that you'll be buying souvenir T-shirts on your trip, wear some of them while you're there, and bring fewer from home.

9 If you're going on a long trip, and you're traveling by car, consider bringing a collapsible hamper. This is a great way to keep your dirty clothes separate.

10 Suitcases with pockets are great for keeping clothes organized. Outer pockets can store dirty clothes for the way home.

HOW TO USE A

HAMMER, WRENCH, AND SCREWDRIVER

Need to fix your scooter, hang a picture, or build a car for the Soap Box Derby? The first step toward becoming a bit handier around the house is to learn what the tools are and how to use them.

HAMMER

Uses: Knocking nails through hard surfaces, such as wood or plaster

Tip: Watch your fingers!

WRENCH

Uses: Tightening or loosening nuts, bolts, and screws

Tips: Use a wrench with the right jaw (or opening) size as the nut or bolt you're working with. Or use an adjustable wrench that allows you to open and close the jaw to fit.

SCREWDRIVER

Uses: Inserting or removing a screw

Tips: There are two main types of screwdrivers—a flat-blade and a Phillips-head. You need to use a screwdriver that matches the head of the screw.

117

HOW TO ACE AN ENGLISH TEST

(by knowing these four tricky grammar rules)

46

2.) Lay or Lie

In the present tense, use lay anytime you mean that someone is putting an object down, and use lie when someone is getting in the right position to take a nap.

For example: Lay your pencil down. Lie on your bed and rest.

1.) Affect or Effect

Affect is a verb and means to cause a reaction. Effect is usually used as a noun that can mean a result or consequence.

For example: The rain might affect what time our plane leaves. What was the effect of adding more milk to the mashed potatoes?

3.) Their or There or They're

Their is possessive and means "belonging to them." There is a location. They're is a contraction of "they are."

For example: Their car is the red one. You can put the groceries over there. They're going to be so excited to see you!

FUNNY ...
I ALWAYS
THOUGHT IT
WAS LION.

4.) Your or You're

Your is possessive and means "belonging to you." You're is a contraction of "you are." Tip: If you get confused, substitute the words, "you are" in the sentence. If it makes sense, use "you're"; if it doesn't, use "your."

For example: Your house is beautiful! You're going to love this chocolate cake.

AFRICA
ANTARCTICA
ASIA
AUSTRALIA
EUROPE
NORTH AMERICA
SOUTH AMERICA

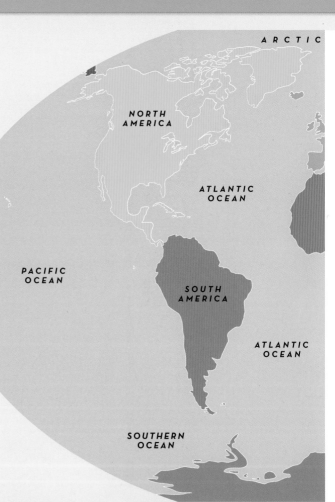

ARCTIC

NORTH
AMERICA

ATLANTIC
OCEAN

PACIFIC
OCEAN

SOUTH
AMERICA

ATLANTIC
OCEAN

SOUTHERN
OCEAN

5 OCEANS ON A MAP OR GLOBE

OCEAN

EUROPE

ASIA

PACIFIC
OCEAN

AFRICA

INDIAN
OCEAN

AUSTRALIA

SOUTHERN
OCEAN

ANTARCTICA

ARCTIC
ATLANTIC
INDIAN
PACIFIC
SOUTHERN

The Southern Ocean is not recognized
by everyone as a separate ocean.
National Geographic defines these
waters as the southernmost parts of
the Atlantic, Indian, and Pacific Oceans.

48

How to check out

BOOKS

at your local

library

It's super easy
(and super fun!).

First, **go to the information desk** at your local library and tell them you'd like to **sign up for a library card.** You'll fill out some paperwork, and then they'll issue you a card.

After that, you'll be able to **borrow books, e-books, even DVDs.**

Just make sure to **pay attention to the date they're due back** at the library. If they are returned late, you may be charged a fine.

Weird but true!

A FEW YEARS AGO, A TINY, 40-BOOK LIBRARY POPPED UP ON A STREET IN NEW YORK CITY. ONLY ONE PERSON COULD FIT INSIDE AT A TIME. IT WAS MADE FROM A RECYCLED PLASTIC WATER TANK, AND IT WAS DESIGNED TO KEEP THE BOOKS SAFE FROM WIND AND RAIN.

49

HOW TO wrap

A present

When you give someone a gift, sure, it's the thought that counts. But it doesn't hurt to make it look pretty, too, *right?*

125

① Roll out enough wrapping paper to cover the present.

② Place the present facedown in the center of the paper. Bring one side of the paper up and over the item, then secure it with a piece of tape. Next, do the same to the other side.

Tip: If there is enough paper, fold the edge of the paper to give it a clean line before taping it.

FIVE Fabulous & Fun
WRAPPING PAPER IDEAS

- THE NEWSPAPER OR SUNDAY COMICS
- SHEET MUSIC
- AN OLD MAP
- PAPER GROCERY BAGS (BONUS POINTS FOR DECORATING IT!)
- A CROSSWORD PUZZLE

3 Face one of the open ends toward you and then bring the left and right sides of paper in toward the center to form flaps out of the paper on the top and bottom.

4 Fold the top flap down and secure it with a piece of tape. Next, fold the bottom flap up and secure it with a piece of tape.

5 Repeat steps 3 and 4 on the other side of the gift. For the finishing touch, if you want, add a ribbon, bow, or gift tag. Voilà! A perfectly wrapped present.

50

How to take care of a pet

Being responsible for a turtle is a little different from caring for a kitty. But there are some basic things you should consider no matter what kind of critter you're parenting. It's a great responsibility to love and care for an animal, but it can definitely be worth the work.

Food & Water

Make sure you know the best kinds of food to feed your pet, and what foods to avoid. Also know how many times a day your pet should eat and the best way to give it water (for example: a bowl or a water bottle).

Home

Be sure that your pet has a safe, clean, and comfortable place to live, play, and sleep.

Exercise

All you fish owners get a pass on this one. But if your pet is one that requires regular exercise, make sure it gets the amount of exercise needed to stay healthy and happy.

Other Care

It's a good idea to get a book or two about the kind of pet you have so that you can become an expert on how to take care of it. Also, you'll want to check in with a veterinarian about caring for your pet. If you have a dog, it needs to be trained. This ensures that both your dog, and the people it encounters, are happy and safe. Be sure to brush and bathe your pet, care for its teeth (if it has any!), and give it lots of love and attention.

How to make comfort food

When you've had a rough day, you're not feeling well, or it's rainy and cold outside, it's nice to know how to make a dish that soothes you. For some people, it's something sweet, like an ice cream sundae. For others, it may be something savory, like dumplings or mashed potatoes.

51

Chicken Noodle Soup

For starters, try this recipe from *NG Kids* magazine. Be sure to get a parent's help to make this cozy favorite.

1 In a large pot, melt 1 tablespoon (14.2 g) of butter with 1 tablespoon (13 g) of olive oil over medium heat.

2 Add 1 cup (50 g) of carrots, 3 stalks of chopped celery, and 1 medium diced onion.

3 Add a pinch of salt and pepper. Cook the mixture for about 10 minutes.

RESEARCHERS HAVE FOUND THAT CHICKEN SOUP HAS ANTI-INFLAMMATORY PROPERTIES, WHICH HELP SOOTHE COLD SYMPTOMS.

4 Add 8 cups (1.9 L) of canned chicken broth and bring the soup to a boil at high heat.

5 Add 3 cups (120 g) of egg noodles, and cook for approximately 9 minutes.

6 Reduce the heat to low, stirring in 3 cups (375 g) of cooked, chopped chicken and a handful of chopped parsley.

7 Cook the soup for 5 more minutes or until the chicken is heated through.

Note: Whenever using knives or sources of heat, make sure an adult is present.

HOW TO

improvise

in any situation

If someone asked you about the most important life skills, improvisation might not exactly be at the top of your list. In fact, you may not even know what it means! But chances are, you probably do it every day. So let's start with the basics. What is it?

In a nutshell, **improvisation means thinking on your feet when you're faced with an unexpected situation.** For example, when a teacher unexpectedly calls on you in class, and you have to come up with a response. When your dad gets a flat tire, and you have to figure out a new way to get to school. Or even when you're hungry but only have three random ingredients in the pantry. But that's not the only kind of improvising.

There's a form of theater, called improv, in which the actors have to react to random scenarios on the spot. **"In improv, performers get an idea from the audience and then use that to make up a performance,"** says Gillian Bellinger, an actor and improv teacher in Los Angeles. For example, in one of Gillian's improv classes, they play a game called slideshow. First, the audience chooses a destination, like Hong Kong, and then two performers use that as a jumping-off point to tell a story, pretending they took a trip there. So, it's sort of like playing make-believe, on the spot, in front of an audience.

It doesn't matter whether you're on stage or on the phone, in front of an audience or in front of your dog, knowing how to adapt and react is super important. Here Gillian shares three important things to remember when improvising on stage—or in life.

52

1 LISTEN. Whenever you're getting new information from someone, listening is crucial. While the other person is talking, try not to think about what you're going to say or ask next. In improv, if you're not listening to your scene partners, then you're not connecting to them and you're not working with them.

2 ACCEPT the reality of the situation. One expression that performers use in improv is, "Yes, and ..."; so, no matter what suggestion the audience gives (You're eating pizza on the moon!), the performer accepts it and then adds new information to it. In life, no matter what pops up during the day, we have to accept it in order to move forward.

3 BE PRESENT. None of us knows what's coming on any given day (or, in improv, in any given moment). Being present helps us not worry about the past or the future. It allows us to focus fully on what's happening right now, so that we create the best possible outcome.

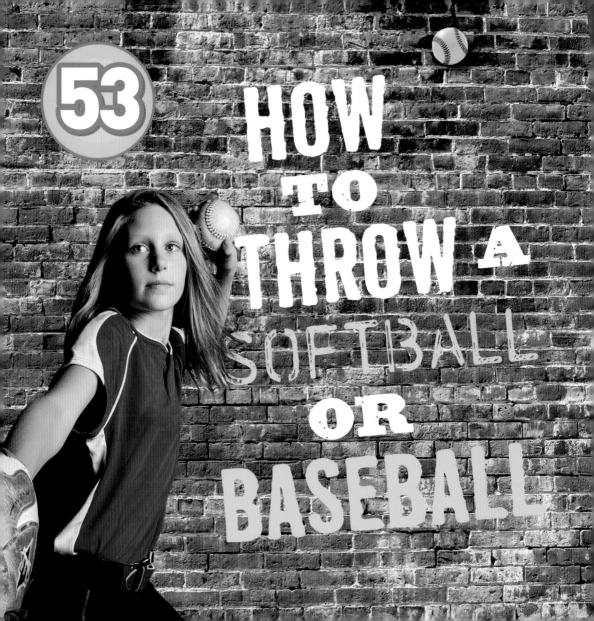

53

HOW TO THROW A SOFTBALL OR BASEBALL

STEP 1 Hold the ball in your dominant hand. For a baseball, place your pointer and middle fingers on the curve of the ball's seam. For a softball, place your pointer, middle, ring (and sometimes pinky, depending on the size of your hand) fingers on the curve of the ball's seam. Then, place your thumb on the underside of the ball, below your pointer finger. You will wear your glove on your nondominant hand.

 STEP 2 Start with your feet shoulder width apart, perpendicular to your target, where you are throwing the ball. If you're right-handed, your left leg is in front and your right foot behind you. If you're left-handed, you turn the other way and put your right leg in front.

 STEP 3 Shift your weight onto your back foot and point your glove at the target.

 STEP 4 Bring the ball over your head, forming a 90-degree angle, or an *L*, with your upper arm and forearm.

 STEP 5 As you start to bring the ball forward, shift the weight of your body forward as well, onto your front leg, and release the ball when it passes by your head.

 STEP 6 As you release the ball, bring your non-throwing arm into the side of your body and your glove to your chest.

54 HOW TO RESPECTFULLY DISAGREE

Whether you disagree with a teacher over a grade you received or **don't see eye to eye** with your lab partner for the science fair project—when someone has an opinion that's different from yours, it can be frustrating. But it's also what makes life interesting! And chances are, you're going to disagree a lot in your lifetime. So it's important to learn how to interact and work with people who think differently. Here are **some tips** for keeping the peace:

Listen. Even if you don't agree with other people's opinions, listen to what they think, how they feel, and why. Instead of trying to change their mind, hear them out—the conversation could be a way for you to learn, too.

Be calm and respectful. Many times, there isn't a right or wrong way of looking at something—there are just different ways. So, instead of saying, "You're wrong," try, "I hear what you're saying, but I don't feel that way."

Know when to drop it. Topics about which people feel passionate can get heated—fast. So, if it seems as if people are having trouble keeping their cool, it's best to end the conversation. You can always say, "It's been great to hear how you feel about this, but I think we should agree to disagree." Then, change the topic to something more lighthearted.

Draw the line at disrespectful. Most of the time, you can walk away. If someone is saying something hurtful or offensive, excuse yourself and take a break.

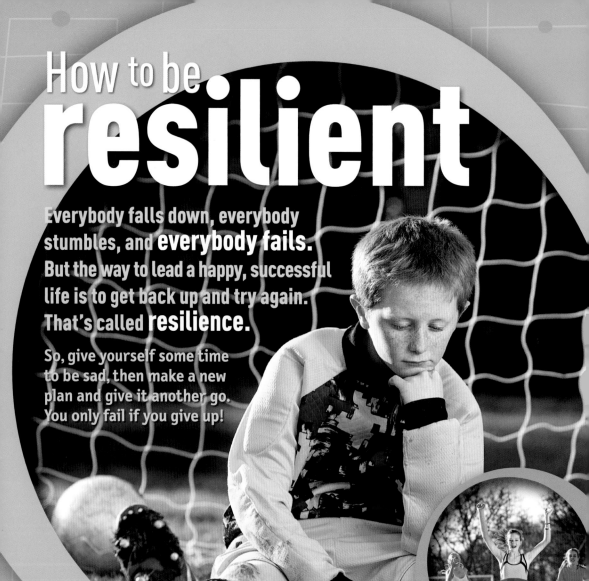

How to be resilient

Everybody falls down, everybody stumbles, and **everybody fails.** But the way to lead a happy, successful life is to get back up and try again. That's called **resilience.**

So, give yourself some time to be sad, then make a new plan and give it another go. You only fail if you give up!

PEOPLE PROFILE: THE WRIGHT BROTHERS

Wilbur and Orville Wright grew up in Dayton, Ohio, U.S.A., in the late 1800s. From a young age, they were **interested in how things** were made.

Wilbur and Orville started a bicycle repair shop. A few years later, they even designed and manufactured their own bicycles. With all that they'd learned, the brothers turned their sights on their true passion—flying.

The brothers studied everything they could find on aeronautics. They looked at other inventors' designs, successes, and failures. Then, they began building kites to test some wings they had designed. When those worked, they moved on to large, piloted gliders.

In 1901, one of their gliders **failed to fly.** The brothers were so discouraged that they predicted no man would fly in their lifetime. But still **they kept plugging away** at their dream. Then, the next year, they successfully flew a piloted glider. And just a year after that, they built and flew the first successful airplane!

Thanks to their **persistence,** the Wright brothers continued to make history with their airplane designs. Today, pilots and aircraft designers still use many of the skills and designs discovered by the Wright brothers.

56

HOW TO BE A GRACIOUS GRACIOUS WINNER AND LOSER

There's nothing like playing a big game—the crowd's cheering, your adrenaline's pumping, your teammates are yelling your name. It can be a struggle to keep a level head when you're charged up and raring to go. But, one surefire way to take the fun out of a game is by being a poor sport—whether you win or lose. Here are some tips to keep your competition friendly and fun.

DON'Ts

- DON'T CALL PEOPLE NAMES, WHINE, POUT, OR GLOAT.

- DON'T HOLD GRUDGES AGAINST OPPONENTS, TEAMMATES, OR EVEN YOURSELF FOR THINGS THAT HAPPEN DURING COMPETITIONS.

- DON'T USE BAD BODY LANGUAGE, EVEN IF AN OFFICIAL MAKES A CALL YOU DON'T LIKE, AND ESPECIALLY AFTER THE GAME—WIN OR LOSE.

DOs

- DO CONGRATULATE THE WINNER EVERY TIME, EVEN IF YOU DON'T FEEL LIKE IT.

- DO PERFORM YOUR BEST AND BE PROUD OF YOUR-SELF, NO MATTER WHAT THE SCOREBOARD SAYS.

- DO ENCOURAGE YOUR TEAMMATES AND OFFER POSITIVE SUPPORT, EVEN WHEN THEY MAKE MISTAKES.

- DO RESPECT THE OFFICIALS' DECISIONS WITHOUT COMPLAINING.

57

HOW TO SPEAK UP

You know that feeling when you have something really great to say, but you're too nervous to raise your hand and say it?

Or, you have a really funny story to tell at lunch, but the second everyone stops talking and looks over at you to listen, you freeze? Public speaking is a really common fear. But with practice, you could be talking to crowds as the class president—or, who knows, the U.S. president!

Jimmy Thai **is a member of** Toastmasters International **(an organization that helps people improve their public speaking and leadership skills) and a founder of** Leadership Foundation Academy.

"I think practicing public speaking is the most important thing people can do for themselves," said Jimmy. "I came to the United States as a refugee from Vietnam. I grew up in a culture where kids were supposed to listen, not talk. It's a privilege to be able to speak up, express your opinions, and use your voice. So, if given the opportunity to speak in front of people, embrace it. You definitely don't want to take it for granted."

Here, Jimmy shares four tips for how to be a master communicator.

1. Choose a topic you care about.

Then become an expert on that subject. If you do your research and you're passionate about the subject, your audience will see how confident and knowledgeable you are about it.

2. Be prepared.

Don't wing it! Anything that is worth doing takes time and effort. Even for a speech that will only last a few minutes, set aside a few hours to prepare.

3. Be yourself.

If you're funny and you like to crack jokes, then go right ahead. But, if you're naturally quiet or more serious, stay focused on your key message. Don't worry about being something you're not. Keep your body language relaxed and confident, and try to view your speech as a conversation with the audience.

4. Practice, practice, practice.

Lots of people feel nervous talking in front of a crowd, but there are things you can do to get more comfortable. Feeling butterflies? Try taking a few deep breaths one to two minutes before you give your speech. Also, try to spend some time in the room, or on the stage, where you'll be presenting to get familiar with the space. The more you can do these things in advance, the calmer you'll be on the day of your presentation.

58

How to pump up your bike tires

There's no reason a flat tire should leave you stranded! Here's a handy lesson on how to be ... well ... handy.

1. Position the tire so that the air valve is on the bottom, near the ground, and take the cap off.

2. Check the side of your bike's tire for its recommended PSI. The PSI (which stands for pound-force per square inch) is the unit of measure for the air pressure in your tires. Every tire has a recommended PSI range, and you don't want to ride on your tires if the pressure is above or below that range.

3. Make sure you have the right kind of pump—it needs to fit your bike's specific valve.

4. Attach the pump to the valve, making sure there's a good seal. (If the tire is not filling with air when you begin pumping, the pump may not be attached properly to the valve.) If there is a lever on the top of the pump, push it down to begin pumping.

5. Pump up your tire a little bit at a time, pausing to check the PSI with an air gauge.

6. When your tire's PSI is within the recommended range, put the cap back on the valve, hop on your bike, and hit the open road!

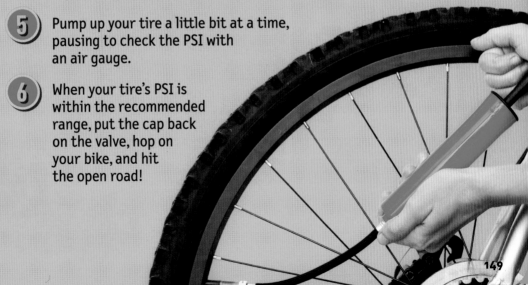

59

HOW TO THROW
A FOOTBALL

STEP 01 HOLD THE BALL IN YOUR DOMINANT HAND WITH YOUR RING AND PINKY FINGERS ON THE LACE, AND YOUR THUMB AROUND THE OPPOSITE SIDE. DON'T GRIP THE BALL TOO TIGHTLY. ALLOW FOR A LITTLE ROOM BETWEEN THE PALM OF YOUR HAND AND THE BALL.

STEP 02

TURN YOUR BODY TO THE SIDE, SO THAT YOUR DOMINANT ARM IS FARTHER FROM YOUR TARGET (AND THE OPPOSITE FOOT IS FORWARD). AND PULL YOUR ARM BACK AT ABOUT SHOULDER/EARLOBE HEIGHT (DON'T SWING YOUR ARM UP HIGH OR DOWN LOW).

STEP 03

WHEN YOU ARE READY TO THROW THE BALL, STEP TOWARD YOUR TARGET, BRING YOUR THROWING ARM FORWARD, AND LET THE BALL SPIN OFF YOUR FINGERS AS YOU RELEASE IT. THE LAST FINGER TO TOUCH THE BALL SHOULD BE YOUR POINTER FINGER, AND THE FOOTBALL SHOULD BE SPINNING IN "A SPIRAL," WITH THE POINTED END OF THE BALL HEADING TOWARD YOUR TARGET AS YOU FOLLOW THROUGH. YOUR BACK LEG WILL COME FORWARD AND YOUR THROWING ARM WILL END AT ABOUT THIGH-LEVEL ON THE OPPOSITE SIDE.

TIP

AT FIRST, DON'T TRY TO THROW IT TOO FAR. INSTEAD, PRACTICE THROWING TO SOMEONE ABOUT 15 OR 20 FEET (ABOUT 5 OR 6 M) AWAY TO GET THE FEEL OF THROWING THE SPIRAL.

60 HOW TO WRITE A PERSONAL STORY

You probably have a **story** that could rival any movie or TV show. Maybe there's something you've experienced that's **funny,** thrilling, inspiring, or **sad.** Your story—the one starring you—deserves to be told! Here are a **few tips** to make readers hang on your every word:

- **Start strong.** Your first paragraph should introduce your story. Start with a statement or scene that grabs the reader's attention.

- **Be concise.** Personal essays can be all different lengths. But to start, try keeping yours to three or four paragraphs.

- **Be descriptive.** You want the reader to be able to picture the situation in his or her mind. So give specific details, such as what the room smelled like, the color of your sweater, what you were feeling, or what it sounded like when you dropped the TV down the stairs.

- **Be organized.** You can experiment with different ways of structuring your story, but a good way to start is by organizing it chronologically, in the order that the events took place.

- **End strong.** Your last paragraph, called the conclusion, is where you wrap up the action of the story, reflect on what you learned from it, and explain how the situation affected you.

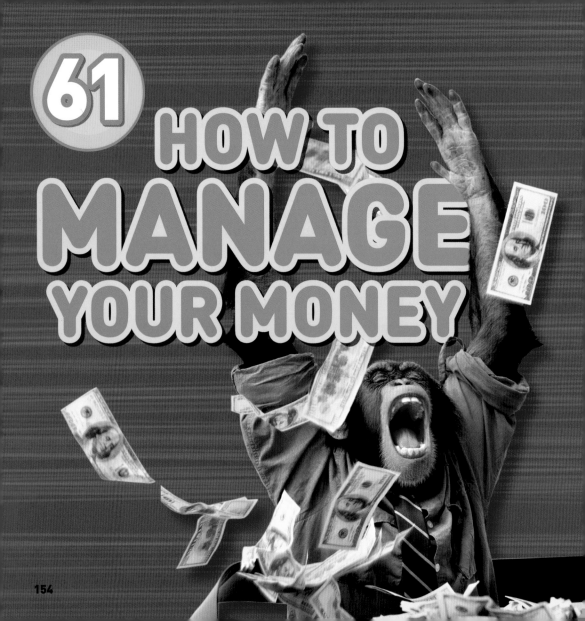

61

HOW TO MANAGE YOUR MONEY

Aside from the $10 you get from Grandma every birthday and the $2 your neighbor gave you for helping her unload groceries ... you might not have much money yet ... or maybe not any at all! But that doesn't mean you can't at least learn how to save it (and spend it wisely when you have it!). So we asked Ron Lieber, a money columnist for the *New York Times* and author of the book, *The Opposite of Spoiled: Raising Kids Who Are Grounded, Generous, and Smart About Money,* for the dish on dough.

> **Here Ron sheds some light on how to get started on your path from rags to riches!**

QUESTION 01

Why is it important to start learning about money when you're young?

Two big reasons. First, when we learn about money, we learn about values. After all, what we spend, where, and how much, says a lot about what we stand for.

Second, college is now terribly expensive if you don't get financial aid (and those numbers will only go up). So you have to be ready for it—and that means having lots of discussions about money starting when you're young.

QUESTION 02

What are some of the best ways to start learning more about money?

Ask Lots of Questions. You should ask whatever you want about money, and adults should answer honestly. Money is a source of mystery and also of power, so of course you're going to have tons of questions about it.

Practice. The best way to learn about money is through practice. And a great way to practice is by getting a regular allowance. You can also ask your parents if you can be responsible for your annual clothing budget. Discuss the clothing you want and need, and what your parents are willing to spend. Then, when you get the lump sum, manage it on your own. But be warned: if you don't budget wisely, you might run out of money, end up with only one pair of jeans, or have to work to earn more for a dress for the school dance. (But spoiler alert: Messing up is part of the learning process.)

What are some of the most important lessons a kid should learn about money before they become an adult?

Saving money requires patience. If you're trying to save your money for something big (like a new bike), you may not be able to buy some of the small things (like a gaming app or even that candy bar) that you want right now. Learning to prioritize a big goal in the future over a little treat now is really important. After all, you can't retire or buy a house without being able to do this.

Consider what makes something worth your money. Know when to spend a little (on things that don't matter much) and when to spend a lot (on things and experiences that deliver a lot of happiness).

Be Generous. Give your money and time to people who are not as lucky as you are, and express gratitude on a regular basis for what you have.

MONEY TALK
Credit Card 101

Here's how a credit card works: When you buy something with one, your bank or credit company pays for it. Then, if you aren't able to pay back all of the money you owe right away, the total amount is divided up and you pay a little back each month. This might seem really great. (I can buy things I don't yet have the money for!) But you also have to pay interest, which is extra money the bank or credit company charges you for borrowing money from them. And watch out: If you are late making one of your monthly payments, you will be charged an additional penalty. So, do your best to pay back the full amount when your payment is due.

How to Press Flowers

1 Find clean, live flowers and pat them dry.

2 Put the flowers between two pieces of parchment paper, printer paper, or cardboard.

3 Place the stack between the pages of a book.

4 Put something heavy on top of the book, like a dumb-bell or a heavier book.

5 Wait two to three weeks, until the flowers are completely dry.

62

weird but true!

FLOWERING PLANTS CALLED MOONFLOWERS BLOOM ONLY AT NIGHT (OR ON OVERCAST DAYS) AND THEN CLOSE AGAIN WHEN THE SUN COMES OUT.

63 HOW TO STUDY

Whether you're a super serious student or follow the "study hard, play harder" school of thought, everyone has their own studious style. And, while it's important to figure out how you study best, here are a few good rules of thumb for everyone.

A Good Space

Have a clean, organized area with enough room to spread out your books, notebooks, flashcards, and other materials.

Peace and Quiet

Most people study best in a place free of distractions, where they can concentrate better.

Enough Time

Make sure you give yourself plenty of time to study. Know how long it takes you to read the material, make your study tools, and go over your notes. It helps to take a break for a few minutes, every half hour or so.

Study Snacks

It's difficult to concentrate with a rumbling stomach. Make sure you have plenty of yummy snacks! Fruit, vegetables, and nuts make the best brain food.

STUDY, SLEEP, <u>AND</u> YOUR BRAIN

Every time you **learn** something new, it carves a tiny path in your brain. Each time you have that same thought, the path gets deeper and deeper and is more likely to **stay with you.** This is why you should **read** something **several times.** Also, while you sleep, your brain goes back through your recent memories, saving the important ones and discarding the unimportant ones. So, **forget pulling an all-nighter** after a serious study session. You **need your sleep** to hold on to what you've learned.

how to
have a
friend
for life

Have your eye on half a BFF necklace? Thinking of going halfsies on a game system? Here's how to make sure your friendships can stand the test of time.

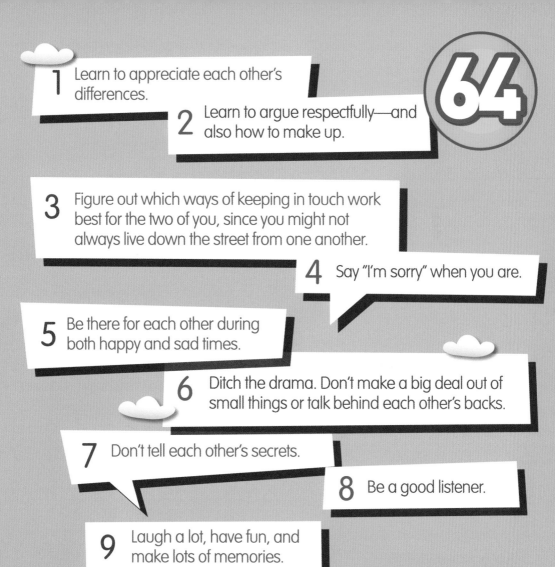

64

1 Learn to appreciate each other's differences.

2 Learn to argue respectfully—and also how to make up.

3 Figure out which ways of keeping in touch work best for the two of you, since you might not always live down the street from one another.

4 Say "I'm sorry" when you are.

5 Be there for each other during both happy and sad times.

6 Ditch the drama. Don't make a big deal out of small things or talk behind each other's backs.

7 Don't tell each other's secrets.

8 Be a good listener.

9 Laugh a lot, have fun, and make lots of memories.

65 How to Relax and De-stress

Relaxation is important. People who stress less are happier, healthier, and live longer than people prone to getting frazzled easily. Everyone should have their own super stress-busting techniques to tap into occasionally.

15 Ideas to Get You Started

1 Go for a walk.

2 Talk to a friend.

3 Watch something that makes you laugh.

4 Write out your feelings in a journal.

5 Exercise.

164

6   Meditate.

7   Read a book, comic book, or magazine.

8   Play with a dog. (Don't have one? Think about volunteering at a shelter!)

9   Help someone who needs it.

10 Paint.

11 Listen to music.

12 Try yoga.

13 Bake.

14 Unplug. (Turn off all devices: your computer, TV, video games, phone, and tablet.)

15 Sit outside in nature.

HOW TO RESPOND
WHEN SOMEONE HURTS
YOUR FEELINGS

IT'S BOUND TO HAPPEN :-(
HERE'S HOW TO HANDLE IT:

- TELL THEM. IT'S GOOD TO BE HONEST ABOUT THE WAY YOU FEEL. YOU COULD SAY, "THAT REALLY HURT MY FEELINGS." IT MIGHT LEAD TO A CONVERSATION THAT WILL HELP YOU UNDERSTAND EACH OTHER BETTER. AND THE OTHER PERSON MIGHT NOT EVEN KNOW THAT WHAT HE OR SHE DID UPSET YOU.

- IGNORE THEM. THIS CAN BE REALLY HARD, BUT IF SOMEONE IS JUST TRYING TO HURT YOU, OR GET A RISE OUT OF YOU, SOMETIMES THE BEST IDEA IS TO COOL DOWN BEFORE YOU RESPOND.

66

- REMEMBER, IT MIGHT NOT BE ABOUT YOU. UNFORTUNATELY, SOMETIMES PEOPLE LASH OUT WHEN THEY'RE HAVING A HARD TIME THEMSELVES. THEY MIGHT HAVE GOTTEN A BAD GRADE ON A TEST, OR MAYBE THEIR DAD YELLED AT THEM BEFORE SCHOOL AND THEN THEY TOOK THEIR FRUSTRATION OUT ON YOU.

- FIND COMFORT IN A FRIEND. IF YOUR FEELINGS ARE HURT, TALK TO SOMEONE YOU CAN TRUST TO BE KIND AND POSITIVE, SUCH AS A FRIEND, SIBLING, OR PARENT.

67

HOW TO PAPIER MÂCHÉ

WHAT YOU'LL NEED...

- One balloon
- A paste mixture made from 2 parts white glue and 1 part water
- Newspaper, torn into strips about 1 to 2 inches (2.5 to 5 cm) wide

- A paintbrush
- More newspaper or a drop cloth to cover your work area

STEP 1 This can be messy, so cover your work area with newspaper or a drop cloth.

STEP 2 Blow up your balloon.

STEP 3

Dip the strips of newspaper into the paste mixture, and use your fingers to squeegee off the extra. Then, lay the strips on the surface of the balloon, trying to keep them flat so that there aren't many ripples or folds.

STEP 4

Cover the entire balloon with three layers of newspaper strips.

the 2011-02 ...ason.

STEP 5

Leave the project to dry for at least one day.

STEP 6

When it's completely dry, you can paint or decorate your creation however you'd like.

HOW TO HIT THE OFF BUTTON

Step away from the screen! Are you someone who is always on your phone or computer or watching TV? It turns out too much screen time isn't just a time suck, it can affect your ability to **concentrate**, sleep well, and even how healthy and happy you feel!

So instead of spending Sunday zoned out on the couch, go have some fun IRL (in real life).

68

Here are **10** real-world boredom-busters.

1 **Get together** with someone in your class you've never hung out with before.

2 Make up a **dance** or write a song with a friend.

3 Set up some objects on your kitchen table, then **sketch** a still life.

4 **Call a grandparent** or a **friend** who lives out of town.

5 Use your imagination to make up a story or **create** a **comic strip.**

6 Go outside. Run, **play** a game, **throw** a ball, or just sit in nature and let your mind **wander.**

7 Put together a **puzzle,** solve a sudoku, or work on a word jumble.

8 Try a **new hobby** you've always thought was cool, like knitting, woodworking, gardening, or cooking.

9 **Read** a book!

10 Sign up to **take a lesson** in a musical instrument you'd like to play!

HOW TO TALK TO ADULTS

Whether you got called to the principal's office, you're looking for a job cutting your neighbors' lawns, or a friend's parent is driving you home, it's good to be able to talk to adults. Here are a few tips that will get them to pay attention. You've got a lot of important things to say!

First, the basics:

- Don't look at your shoes or off into space. If you're talking to adults (or anyone, really), look them in the eyes.

- When you address an adult, use his or her last name and the appropriate title: Mr., Ms., Dr., Lieutenant, etc.

- Shake a person's hand when you're introduced.

- Be polite—don't interrupt or use rude language or slang. Say "please" and "thank you." Replace "yeah" with "yes."

NOW THE ABC'S OF CHITCHAT

69

<u>A</u>sk questions. Do you know where they work? Where they grew up? Do they play an instrument? How about sports? People love talking about themselves, and by asking questions, it shows you're interested in what they have to say.

<u>B</u>e yourself. Remember, they were kids once, too, so don't feel nervous or intimidated. They're probably very interested in what you have to say. Just relax and let your naturally awesome self shine through!

<u>C</u>ontinue practicing. Talking to other people gets easier with practice. The more you do it, the less difficult it will become.

70 How to **handle** yourself **online**

Ah, the World Wide Web. It's a magical place filled with funny **cat videos**, friendship connections, movies, music videos, **games**, and everything else you can think of. You learn **cool things**, see **cool sites**, and find all sorts of things that **inspire** and **entertain** you. But as wonderful as the Internet is, it can also be a place where people **behave badly** and mistakenly think that there are no consequences.

Larry Magid, CEO of ConnectSafely.org, shares the Dos and Don'ts of the World Wide Web.

No one can be 100 percent safe using any powerful technology. But to be safer, you need to understand what is okay to post and what isn't. You have to protect your reputation and also stay away from people online, and off, who are mean or threatening in some way.

What are some ways someone can stay safe online?

What are some examples of things people should not do online?

People should avoid posting anything that could embarrass them or get them into trouble now or in the future. You should be careful about any images you post. Respect your own privacy, as well as other people's privacy. Also, be aware of any apps that report your location or share other personal information with others.

5 more tips for cyber safety

Adapted from "Tips for Strong Secure Passwords" at ConnectSafely.org.

1 Passwords are private

Passwords are private. **Don't share** your passwords, even with friends. It's hard to imagine, but **friendships change,** and you don't want to be impersonated by anyone. Pick a password you can **remember**, but that no one else can guess. One trick: Create a sentence like "I graduated from King School in 05" for the password "IgfKSi05."

2 Read between the lines

It **may be fun** to chat with people all around the world, but be aware that while some people are nice, **others act** nice because **they're trying to get something**.

3 Avoid in-person meetings

To be 100 percent safe, don't meet anyone in person. If you really have to get together with someone you "met" online, **don't go alone**. Have the meeting in a public place, tell a parent, and **bring some friends** along.

4 Be nice online

Or at least treat people the way you'd want to be treated. People who are **nasty** and **aggressive** online are at greater risk of being **bullied** or harassed themselves. If someone's mean to you, **try not to react**. Definitely **don't retaliate**, and talk to a trusted adult or a friend who can help. **Use privacy tools** to block the meanies.

5 Think about what you post

Sharing personal photos or details about your life online, even in private emails, can **cause problems** for you later on. Even people you consider friends can **use this info against you**, especially if they become ex-friends.

How to impress at a party

5 Tips to Remember

1 Before you arrive, think of a few cool things you can talk to anyone about, such as a new pet, a recent trip, or a school project you're working on.

2 When meeting people for the first time, smile and introduce yourself. If you're meeting a friend's parents, you might want to shake their hand.

3 Need to introduce two people to one another? Here's an easy rule of thumb: Speak first to the person who is older (if you're introducing an adult), or with whom you're less familiar (if you're introducing peers). For example, you'd likely turn to your teacher, your friend's parent, or your grandmother first, and say something like, "Mrs. Grant, I'd like to introduce you to my friend, Alison." Then turn to your friend and say, "Alison, this is my teacher, Mrs. Grant."

4 If you're eating, be polite. Chew with your mouth closed, and don't talk with pizza in your mouth.

5 Pay the host a compliment. Even if the party's a bit of a dud, be specific about something you appreciate (such as the food, music, or decorations). Also, be sure to say "Thank you" to the host before you leave.

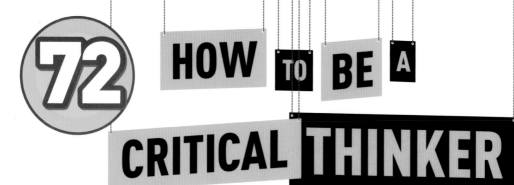

72 HOW TO BE A
CRITICAL THINKER

So, first things first: What does it mean to think critically? It means **analyzing information** that you're given instead of just accepting that it's true. It's important to think critically whenever you're being asked to believe anything—whether it's something you see on social media or in a commercial, hear on the news, or read in a book or newspaper. You should always be trying **to figure out if the** information is accurate.

182

HERE ARE A FEW QUESTIONS TO GET YOU THINKING CRITICALLY:

Q? Who created this article/advertisement/news segment/Internet post, etc.?

Q? Where did the creator of this message get the information?

Q? What is the creator of this message trying to get me to believe?

Q? Is the creator of this message trying to get me to buy something? If so, what?

Q? Do I have any reason to trust, or believe, the person who's giving me this information?

Q? Does this information make sense to me? Or does something feel off about this message?

Q? How can I check the facts, get more information, and draw my own conclusion?

73

HOW TO EXERCISE

No, we're not talking about walking laps to kill time in gym class. When you really get into it, exercise is kind of **magical.** It can make you **healthier, happier,** and **less stressed.** It can help you **sleep more soundly, concentrate** better, and even **fight illness.** You should aim to get at least one hour of physical **activity** a day. So, find something you **love doing,** and make it a habit **now.**

IT DOESN'T HAVE TO BE BORING! HERE ARE SOME FUN IDEAS TO GET YOU ... *MOVING*

1 Go kayaking or canoeing.

2 Running too ho-hum? Pump up the jams to get you going.

3 Go sledding.

4 Play a sport, such as soccer, ice hockey, or tennis.

5 Learn something new, like fencing or curling.

6 Go hiking—don't forget to bring a camera!

7 Swim—time yourself doing a lap and then try to beat it!

8 Put on your raincoat, grab an umbrella and boots, and take a rain walk!

9 Ride a horse.

10 Take an agility training course with your dog.

HOW TO BE AN ADVENTUROUS EATER

It usually starts simple enough: You get invited to eat at a friend's house. You all sit down, dinner is served, and then you see it. You know it's food, because you recognize it from somewhere ... But, it's not something you eat at home, and it's definitely not something you've tasted.

SO, WHAT DO YOU DO NEXT?

Just go ahead, **try it**! It's natural that the foods your family eats are the ones you're most comfortable with, but there are all kinds of new delicious dishes to discover. Consider yourself a culinary explorer.

STEP 1
Don't say, **Ewww!** No matter what it is. Remember to be respectful of whoever made it.

STEP 2
Ask the person serving the food the **best way to eat it**. Do you need to peel it first? Is it best dipped in butter? Should you add salt and pepper?

STEP 3
Keep an **open mind**. It may become your new favorite food.

STEP 4
Start small. Just **take a little** bite at first, and work your way up to a heaping spoonful.

STEP 5
It's totally fine not to like something. But instead of saying, "That was gross," you could say, **"Thank you. I'm glad I tried it!"**

weird but true!

POPULAR PIZZA TOPPINGS VARY FROM PLACE TO PLACE. IN JAPAN, YOU MIGHT HAVE MAYONNAISE OR SEAWEED ON YOUR PIZZA; IN GERMANY, CANNED TUNA IS A POPULAR TOPPING; AND IN AUSTRALIA, YOU CAN ORDER YOUR PIZZA TOPPED WITH CROCODILE!

How to Carve a Pumpkin

75

1. First, find your jack-o'-lantern style. Do you like yours scary? Or silly? Are you into plain, smiling pumpkins or ones with more pizzazz?

2. Ask an adult to help you. Cut a large circle from the top or bottom of your pumpkin.

4. Use a pencil or marker to draw your design on the outside of your pumpkin.

3. Roll up your sleeves and scoop out the slimy seeds and strings from the inside of your pumpkin.

5. Then, ask an adult to carve along the lines you drew, or buy a kid-friendly carving kit and carefully do it yourself.

6. Place a small candle or battery-operated tea light inside of your pumpkin, so that light shines through the holes.

7. Display your glowing gourd in a window or in the front of your house for everyone to see!

189

How to let your imagination run WILD

76

Kickstarter is one of the websites where creators go when they have a **great idea** but don't yet have the **funds** to make it a reality. They put their project on the website and ask people who see its potential to contribute money. So many cool projects begin at Kickstarter—movies, music, comic books, science experiments, art installations, inventions, and more. But there's one thing they all have in common: They began as **a little spark in someone's imagination.**

"I think imagination is being able to see something that's **not been seen before**," says Victoria Rogers, the art and photography outreach lead at Kickstarter. "It's about **introducing a new idea** to the world."

Here, Victoria shares her TIPS on how to let YOUR imagination run WILD.

Let Your Mind Wander. And give yourself plenty of time to explore. That might mean just taking out a blank piece of paper and seeing what comes of it.

Be Inspired by Other Great Ideas. Read about what other people are doing. Let their ideas inspire you and help your ideas grow and develop.

Don't Be Afraid to Fail. Failure is normal. But the fear of it is one of the biggest things that can hold you back. There's value in what you learn from failing, and there's value in coming back and trying again.

Be Encouraging of Others. Support people who are brave enough to put an idea out there.

Check out a few of Victoria's **favorite** Kickstarter projects:

The Birthday Cake Project
A woman in New Orleans, Louisiana, U.S.A., S. Louise Neal, wanted to bake a birthday cake for someone every day in June. She said, "A birthday is an opportunity to pause and celebrate life," and she wanted to share that joy with people. So, she raised funds to make the cakes, and she delivered them to people all around New Orleans.

Painting for Satellites
Artist Molly Dilworth wanted to see what it would be like to paint things that were so massive they could be viewed from above by satellites. So she painted entire rooftops in New York City. It was an ambitious, imaginative project.

Balloon Mapping Kit
The Public Laboratory for Open Technology and Science wanted to take images of the world from above by attaching cameras to big balloons. These images help map places in the world that are very hard to get to or take aerial images of. The cameras take multiple pictures of the area, and then, by laying the pictures on top of one another, you get a full view of the landscape. Even more exciting is that the group made kits you can buy, so you can do it yourself in your own neighborhood.

77 HOW TO BUILD AN AWESOME PILLOW FORT

BECAUSE ... WHY NOT?

WHAT YOU'LL NEED:

- **HEAVY OBJECTS** TO HOLD THE BLANKETS OR SHEETS IN PLACE (LIKE BOOKS, SHOES, OR TOYS)

- **FURNITURE** LIKE CHAIRS, COUCHES, AND SIDE TABLES TO FORM THE WALLS

- **LIGHTWEIGHT BLANKETS OR SHEETS** TO DRAPE OVER FURNITURE TO MAKE ROOFS AND/OR DOORS

- **COUCH CUSHIONS,** WHICH CAN BE STACKED OR STOOD ON THEIR SIDES, TO USE AS WALLS OR DOORS

STEP 1: START CONSTRUCTING AND GO WILD!

HOW TO START A CLUB

Decide on a theme. It could be comic books, gardening, comedy, or yoga— whatever interests **you.**

Pick a **day** and a **time** to meet. Maybe once a month or even once a week.

Ask some friends who share the **same interest** to be in the club.

Spread the word! Use **social media** to advertise your club—or just put flyers up around school so that **new members** will know how to join.

78

Be open to new ideas about how to improve or grow the club. And **have fun!**

Figure out **what you'll do** when you meet. Is it more of a discussion club, or do you **participate** in activities together?

197

79

How to Make NEW Friends

It's pretty great to have someone you can **laugh with** until milk comes out of your nose. Someone who likes to **hang out** and do the things you like to do, and whom you can talk to about your **secret crush.** So, if you're in the market for a **new bud,** here are some strategies for **meeting** new people who might also make **great friends!**

Go places or **join groups** where there are other people your age who have similar interests. For example, do you like nature and being outdoors? Join a hiking group or attend an outdoorsy summer camp.

Spend time with people around whom you can be yourself. It's not fun pretending to be someone you're not, just to get along with the crowd.

Choose good, kind people to hang around. Friends make you happy, are fun to be around, and inspire you to be the best version of yourself.

If you're shy, work on introducing yourself. Have a few questions prepared to ask when you meet someone new.

Be the kind of friend you'd like to have. If you want to *have* a good friend, you need to *be* a good friend.

HOW TO LOOK ON THE BRIGHT SIDE

80

Sometimes, bad **things happen** that we can't control. But we can control how we react to the situation. Next time something gets you down, try looking for "the good." The good could be small, like getting some fresh air and exercise after your car broke down. Or it could be big, such as making a **new friend** while trying out for the soccer team, even though you didn't make it. The point is, there is always some good to be found. You just have to **find it**.

➡️ Instead of thinking about all of the things that could go wrong, ask yourself what could **go right.**

➡️ Is there **anything** to be learned from the bad situation? Focus on any lessons that may have come from it.

➡️ Sure, you had a bad day. But there's someone, somewhere, who probably **had it worse.** Find something to do that could help that person and make their day brighter.

➡️ Remember, no matter what happened today, tomorrow is a **new day.** And you have the power to make it great!

How to BREAK a bad habit

We all have them. Here's how to get rid of them:

1 Make your goal official. **Tell someone about it or write it down in a journal or notebook. Support from others really helps to make a change in your behavior.**

2 **Usually, we've started a habit because we** get something **from it, such as** comfort, distraction, **or** pleasure. **Try to figure out when you usually indulge in the habit and what you're feeling at the time. For example: Do you bite your nails when you get nervous or maybe when you're bored watching TV?**

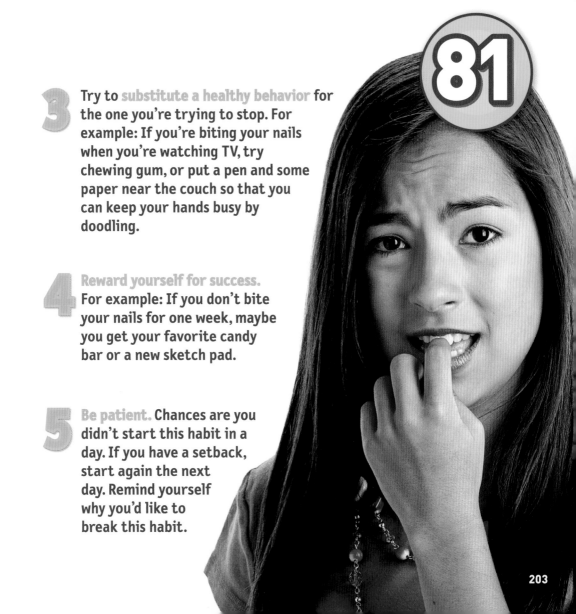

3 Try to **substitute a healthy behavior** for the one you're trying to stop. For example: If you're biting your nails when you're watching TV, try chewing gum, or put a pen and some paper near the couch so that you can keep your hands busy by doodling.

4 Reward yourself for success. For example: If you don't bite your nails for one week, maybe you get your favorite candy bar or a new sketch pad.

5 Be patient. Chances are you didn't start this habit in a day. If you have a setback, start again the next day. Remind yourself why you'd like to break this habit.

81

How **you** can help
SAVE the PLANET

82

Mother Nature sure has been good to us. She's given us trees to climb, oceans to swim in, and lizards that walk on water. But we have to watch how our behavior affects the Earth. Our trash, our food choices, how much energy we use—all of that has a major impact on the environment. And the more you learn about it, the more you can do to help.

HERE ARE 10 WAYS YOU CAN HELP, TODAY!

1. Recycle.
2. Use less water.
3. Carpool, and walk or ride your bike when you can.
4. Donate old toys, clothes, and other household items instead of throwing them away.

5 Reduce food waste by eating leftovers and making use of items you already have in the fridge.

6 Try to eat fruits and vegetables that are in season and were grown locally.

7 Use reusable water bottles and grocery bags.

8 Turn off all your electronics, including TVs and computers, at night.

9 Don't litter!

10 Get involved in a local environmental group.

weird but true!

IT'S ESTIMATED THAT PEOPLE AROUND THE WORLD USE ENOUGH TOILET PAPER EACH DAY TO EQUAL 27,000 TREES.

83

DISCOVER WHERE YOU CAME FROM

Your family history might sound like a bit of a "snoozefest" now ... but it's actually a cool way to become your own family detective. And one day, you'll be glad you know your own family's story.

- Start by asking your parents and grandparents to help you fill out a family tree.

- Then ask about the people on the family tree. Try questions like where they were born, if they moved here from another country, what they did for work, and if they had any hobbies.

- Ask to see any pictures or mementos from earlier generations.

- Find out if any members of your family have looked into your family's history and what they found.

- Ask your parents about using a service that helps trace your ancestry and what parts of the world your family came from.

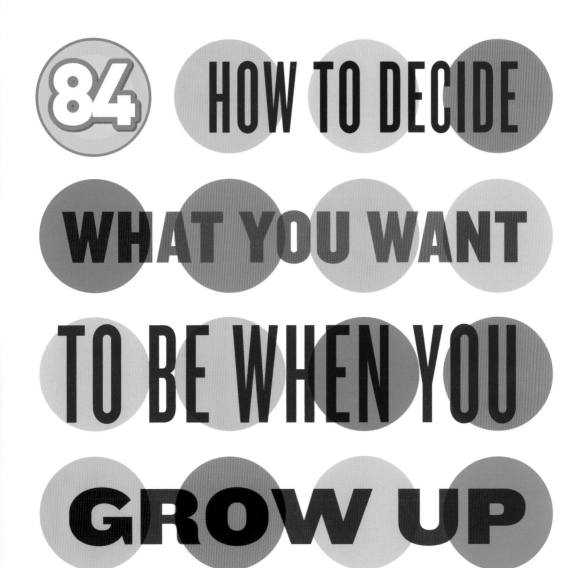

84 HOW TO DECIDE WHAT YOU WANT TO BE WHEN YOU GROW UP

When the founders of **Roadtrip Nation** graduated from college in 2001, they weren't sure what they wanted to do next. So, they set off on a cross-country road trip (in a bright green RV!) to interview professionals who had turned their **passions into careers**. On that first trip, they interviewed people like the **CEO of Starbucks**, a director for *Saturday Night Live,* a stylist for **Madonna**, and even a lobsterman from **Maine**. Since then, Roadtrip Nation has interviewed hundreds of leaders to help inspire young people to forge their own professional paths.

Here, Jason Manion of **Roadtrip Nation** shares tips for how to find answers to the question:

WHAT DO I WANT TO DO WHEN I GROW UP?

Go on a job hunt. Make it your mission to learn about as many different kinds of careers as you can. Ask adults what their jobs are and what a typical day is like for them. And, if you want to hear more about cool careers like a Zen master, human rights attorney, or hip-hop mogul, visit roadtripnation.com.

Identify your interests. Try not to get hung up on the exact title of what you'd like to be. Instead, think about the things you'd like to do. Do you like working with your hands? Do you like music? Helping people? Science? What makes you happy?

Make every day count. Try to do something every day to nurture whatever it is you're interested in. Need some ideas?
- Take a class at your community center on something you're interested in.
- Read a book by someone in a career that you'd like to know more about.
- Find people who do something really cool and follow them on Instagram or Twitter.

Think broader. You don't have to be just one thing. You can find jobs that mix many of your interests together. Love music and law? You could be a music lawyer. Like science and sports? You could be a professional trainer or work in sports medicine.

Shout it from the rooftops. Once you figure out something you're passionate about, tell everyone! The more people you talk to about your interests, the more likely you'll be to find people to talk to who work in that industry.

Get out of your comfort zone. Be bold! Whether it's asking to interview someone with a cool job, or calling a local business to see if they have volunteer opportunities, push yourself to have new experiences. You can learn a lot about yourself and the kind of life you want to have by trying new things.

Want to interview a leader you look up to?
Here are some questions to get you started:

- **HOW** did you find this **CAREER** and/or your passion?
- What **OBSTACLES** did you have to overcome and **HOW** did you do that?
- How do you define **SUCCESS?**

 211

85

HOW TO DEAL WITH JEALOUSY

Face it. Whether it's your best friend's **brand-new phone** or your brother's **first place** basketball trophy, **we've all been jealous**—feeling like someone else has something we want. Jealousy makes you **feel** pretty **horrible,** and it may cause you to do or say things you don't mean. Next time you're feeling jealous, check out these ways to defeat the **green-eyed monster.**

ONE It's important to **recognize** when you're feeling jealous. Sometimes, just **acknowledging it helps** you get over the jealousy faster.

TWO **Think** about whether there are steps you could be taking to bring the things you want into your life. **Make a list** of your goals and your plans to achieve them.

THREE Think kind, compassionate thoughts about the person you are jealous of.

FOUR Sit for a few minutes and **think** about all the things that are good in your life and for which you are grateful.

How to train a DOG to do a TRICK

Teach a Dog to Sit

1. Show your dog a **treat** and hold it just a little above his head. If your dog jumps up for the treat, you are holding it too far away.

2. Say **"Sit"** as you move the treat a little higher above your dog's head. As he looks up, he will naturally lower his haunches and sit.

3. When your dog sits, give him the treat and lots of **praise.**

4. Encourage your dog to **stand** up, then repeat steps 1–3, until your dog is moving into a sitting position easily when you say "Sit" and raise the treat.

86

5   Now **do steps 1–3 again,** but this time with your empty hand. If your dog still follows your hand and sits, give him a treat (from your other hand or pocket) and lots of praise.

6   As your dog begins to master this trick, gradually lessen the amount of movement you make with your hand when you say "Sit." Also, begin **putting the treat farther away,** in another room or on a table nearby. But when your dog does sit, keep giving him lots of praise and the treat.

7   Pretty soon, your dog will follow the command without seeing the treat or you moving your hand. **Congratulations!** You're a dog trainer extraordinaire.

HOW TO HANDLE A KNIFE SAFELY

Handling knives can be dangerous. You must always **be alert** and careful when using a knife. Once you've gotten permission to proceed from your parents, here are **some tips** for staying safe while channeling your inner chef.

➡ Your work area should be **waist level.** If you're not tall enough, use a sturdy step stool.

➡ Use a **large cutting board,** so that your cutting area isn't cramped.

➡ Instead of keeping your fingers outstretched on the hand holding the food, **curl them under** like a C-shaped claw.

➡ Keep your fingers out of the way of the blade, **focus,** and practice cutting slowly.

➡ Make sure your knife is **sharp.** Using a dull knife can be more dangerous because you have to push down harder and it can slip from the object you're trying to cut.

When carrying a knife, **carry it by its handle**, with the tip **facing down**.

If a knife falls off the counter, move out of its way and let it fall. **Never** try to **catch** a falling knife.

87

HOW TO SOLVE PROBLEMS

Problems come in all siZes. Some are **BIG,** like getting locked out of the house after school. And some are pretty small, like running out of milk for your cereal. But one thing's for sure: There will come a time when you'll need to know how to handle a sticky situation. When that time comes, it's important to stay *calm* and levelheaded while you consider the possible solutions.

NEXT TIME YOU'RE STUCK, GIVE THIS A TRY:

88

01 Identify the problem.

02 Make a list of possible solutions. Try to think outside the box.

03 Consider the outcomes of each of the possible solutions and weigh the risks involved against the potential rewards.

04 Choose a solution and try it.

05 Were you successful in solving the problem? Think about why your solution did, or did not, work. If you need to, go back to step 2 and consider trying a different solution.

06 Don't give up. As the old proverb says, "If at first you don't succeed, try, try again!"

weird but true!

THE WORLD RECORD FOR SOLVING A RUBIK'S CUBE IS 39.579 SECONDS. THOSE ARE SOME LIGHTNING-FAST FINGERS!

One of the easiest ways is by learning one of the songs that list all 50 states. You can learn them alphabetically in "Fifty Nifty United States," or geographically from west to east in the "50 States Song." You can find both the lyrics and full songs online.

Then, **learn where each state is** on the **map.**

Washington

M o n

Oregon

Idaho

Nevada

Utah

California

Arizona

Hawai'i

200 miles

Alaska

400 miles

Montana
North Dakota
Minnesota
Wisconsin
Michigan
South Dakota
Wyoming
Iowa
Nebraska
Illinois
Indiana
Ohio
Colorado
Kansas
Missouri
New Mexico
Oklahoma
Arkansas
Kentucky
Tennessee
Texas
Mississippi
Alabama
Georgia
Louisiana
Florida
South Carolina
North Carolina
Virginia
West Virginia
Pennsylvania
New York
Maine
Vermont
New Hampshire
Massachusetts
Rhode Island
Connecticut
New Jersey
Delaware
Maryland
Washington, D.C.

200 miles

HOW TO TELL YOUR LEFT FROM YOUR RIGHT

Sure, this is something you learned when you were younger, but lots of people still confuse left and right well into adulthood. So, here's a simple trick: When you put your pointer and thumb fingers out on your left hand, it makes an *L*.

90

❤ for Left

How to be tolerant

The more people you meet, the more you'll begin to notice that *not everyone is just like you.* They may not have grown up like you or have a family like yours. They might not believe the same things, and they might not have the same opinions. And, while at first that might be frustrating, or even a little unsettling, it's actually pretty cool. The world would be bland if we were all the same. And, we learn a lot—about ourselves and about others—by getting to know people who are different from us.

Being tolerant means getting comfortable with people who live, believe, and think *differently* than you do. It doesn't mean that your beliefs are any less strong. Tolerance just means that you *practice compassion* toward others, and that you appreciate *diversity,* both in people and their ideas.

> **"** *In the practice of tolerance, one's enemy is the best teacher.* **"**
> —the Dalai Lama

91

How to

92 QUIET

Your
MIND

Maybe you need to focus, you're feeling anxious, or your thoughts are racing. *(I need to study for my science test! I forgot my music for band practice! I hope Emma isn't mad at me!)* One way to calm your mind and body is by practicing mindfulness. MindUP is a program that teaches students about mindfulness.

Try this activity from MindUP to quiet your mind:

1. Sit with your feet on the floor, your hands loosely in your lap, and your shoulders relaxed. Close your eyes or just look down at your hands.

2. Begin with slow, deep breaths, pulling air up and into your belly. Bring all your attention to the sensation of your breath, moving in and out.

3 If your mind wanders, simply bring your attention back to your breath.

4 Continue for a few minutes, noticing the quiet, empty space between you and your thoughts.

5 When you are ready, slowly open your eyes and bring your attention back to the room.

Jennifer Erickson

is a teacher in Vancouver, British Columbia, Canada, and she's been teaching the MindUP curriculum for years.

Q: What does mindfulness mean?

A: To practice mindfulness, you focus and concentrate on something that's happening right now — like your breath, a sound, a taste, or even a smell.

Q: Why is it important to be mindful?

A: It's a way to train your brain and body to respond to stress. It can help you concentrate in class, feel less anxious, respond to conflicts more thoughtfully (instead of reacting with anger or aggression), help you sleep better, increase compassion, and could even make you happier!

How to Choose the Perfect Gift

Even if you can't buy the latest and greatest gadget or front-row tickets to an awesome concert, you can still pick a really **wow-worthy present.** Great gifts are personal and let the recipients know you were thinking about who they are and what **makes them happy.** People love when you remember something they said they like months ago or a silly inside joke you share. So, when picking out primo presents, start by considering these questions.

What are some of their favorite things?

What do they love— what are their passions or hobbies?

Is there something you enjoy doing together?

Is there a memento from a fun time you shared together?

Have they mentioned something recently that they wish they had or would like to try?

93

94

HOW TO TAKE A GREAT YEARBOOK PHOTO

If you're lucky, when you look back at your school pictures over the years, you'll have some that are cute (Look at those pigtails and missing teeth!), a few that are funny (What was I thinking with that haircut?), and lots that make you smile (Oh, I remember that shirt—I scored my first soccer goal in it!). But no matter what, a great school picture is a reminder of who you were that year.

Sarah Smith and Kelvin Miller are from Lifetouch, a photography company that has been taking school pictures for 80 years. Here, they share their top tips for taking a smile-worthy snap.

Choose an outfit that makes you **feel great**, maybe one that you've gotten compliments on in the past.

You, your **eyes**, and your **smile** are the star of the show, not your clothes. So don't wear anything that's really busy— like a loud pattern or bright neon—that will steal attention away from your face.

Don't over-practice your smile. The longer a smile is on your face, the less authentic it is. Try thinking about something that makes you laugh—maybe a joke or something silly a friend said—to make your smile look sincere.

Try **not to get your hair cut** less than two weeks before picture day. That way it will have grown out to look more natural.

- Consider **matching your top to your eye color.** The repetition of colors will make your eyes pop!

- When you sit down to take your photo, **sit up straight** and make your back tall.

- If you're feeling nervous or tense, **try yawning.** This will relax all the muscles in your body, helping you to feel—and look—a bit more natural.

- **Listen** to the photographers. They're trying to get you into a posture that meets your yearbook needs. Just because you feel funny, doesn't mean you won't look great.

- **Be yourself.** This picture is not only for the yearbook, it's for your friends and family—people who love you. So just be you!

Need outfit inspiration? Check out this elementary school teacher, Dale Irby, from Richardson, Texas, U.S.A., who wore the same clothes for picture day, every year, for 40 years. Proof that a sense of humor never goes out of style!

235

95

How to LOAD the DISHWASHER

You've seen your parents do it a million times, but still it's a mystery. What are all those prongs? Why can't you just place the cups right-side up? Won't the knives and forks fall through the holes in the racks? All good questions. And, at long last, here are some answers.

Try not to stack or overlap dishes to the point where water won't be able to reach their surfaces.

Position bowls, cups, and glasses upside down in the racks so that the water, which shoots upward from the bottom of the dishwasher, can reach the dirtiest parts of the dishes.

Usually glasses, cups, serving bowls, saucepans, and large utensils go on the top rack.

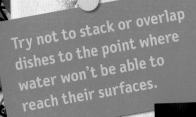

Mostly plates, platters, cookie sheets, mixing bowls, and larger pots and pans go on the bottom rack.

Utensils go in their own basket, which sits on one of the racks. For safety, it's best to load forks and knives facing downward.

How to shine like the STAR you are

Do you have **big, wild hair?** Or a **loud, silly laugh?** Do you like to **sing opera?** Or are you a master at **impressions?** We all have qualities that make us special and unique. Sometimes, though, it can be hard to show people the parts of our personality that might make us different from the norm. But it's *the things that set us apart that are also what make us special.* So embrace all the things about you—all the quirks, all the crazy bits—that make you, **YOU!**

"Why fit in when you were born to stand out?"
— *Dr. Seuss*

"To be yourself in a world that is constantly trying to make you something else is the greatest accomplishment."
— *Ralph Waldo Emerson*

"Always be a first rate version of yourself and not a second rate version of someone else."
— *Judy Garland*

"Baby, you're a firework. Come on let your colors burst."
— *Katy Perry*

96

97 HOW TO TELL SOMEONE YOU LIKE LIKE THEM

1. Make eye contact.

2. Smile at this person.

3. Ask about things you know are important to this person, such as an upcoming swim meet or a new issue of his or her favorite comic book.

4. Let this person know about an event you'll be attending, like a basketball game after school. Then say, "You should come, too," or "I hope you'll be there."

5. Put a "just because" note in this person's locker.

6. If you see something that made you think of him or her, say so!

7. Give a compliment. If you like this person's singing voice, the poem he wrote in class, or her new sweatshirt, say so.

8. Bring an extra treat in your lunch to share with this person.

9. Ask him to dance at the school dance, or do something nice for her on Valentine's Day.

10. If you're feeling brave and the moment feels right, just tell this person how you feel!

240

How to soothe a burn, beesting, and mosquito bite

Be the summer camp superstar when you heal the wounds of fellow campers.

For **minor burns** from touching something **hot**, hold the affected area under **cool** (not super cold) water until the pain goes away. (And grab a magazine. It could take a while.)

When **stung by a bee**, remove the **stinger** with your fingers or tweezers, without squeezing the area, which can spread the venom. **Elevate** the stung body part if possible, and **apply ice** to the sting. If the area itches, apply **calamine lotion** or a mixture of **baking soda and water**.

If you get bitten by a **mosquito**, try your best **not to scratch**. Scratching can break the skin, which can lead to **infection**. To help calm the itchiness of a bug bite, apply **calamine lotion** or an **ice pack**.

If you or your friend are allergic to beestings, find an adult or doctor right away.

243

99 How to let go of REGRET

You might feel bad about something you did or said in the past that hurt someone. Or maybe you behaved in a way that wasn't true to who you are. It's good to recognize when you've done something wrong or something that you don't feel good about. But instead of stewing in regret, figure out the best way to move forward.

Is there someone you can apologize to? Is there something you can do to make sure you don't make the same mistake again?

If so, do these things. Instead of feeling bad about what happened in the past, try to use the experience to become a better version of you.

HOW TO MAKE YOURSELF HAPPY

A big part of growing up is becoming the expert on all things **YOU.** It's good to know, for example, if reading in the car makes you feel sick or eating chocolate ice cream makes you bounce off the walls. It's good to know, too, if sitting in the front of the classroom helps you concentrate or if hanging out with a certain friend lifts your spirits. And it's super important to **KNOW WHAT MAKES YOU HAPPY.**

When you've had a **bad day** or you're **feeling down,** do the things you know are good for you: The things that calm you, make you laugh, and remind you that everything is going to be okay.

HAPPY QUIZ

1 I always **laugh** when I watch/read   .

2 Talking to   always makes me **feel better.**

3 My favorite kind of **mood-boosting** exercise is   .

4 I feel **coziest** when I   .

5 My favorite way to **relax** is   .

6 My favorite **inspirational quote** is   .

7 A **song** that always pumps me up is   .

8 I could happily **spend hours**   .

9 The way I prefer to get my **feelings** out is   .

10 I always have **fun** when I   .

These are just to get you started. What else makes you happy?

KEEP THE LIST GOING!

CHECKLIST

- ☐ How to make snow ice cream
- ☐ How to say "I'm sorry"
- ☐ How to fold origami
- ☐ How to help someone who's choking
- ☐ How to conduct an experiment
- ☐ How to have thicker skin
- ☐ How to make an edible gift
- ☐ How to pump gas
- ☐ How to write a check
- ☐ How to resolve conflict peacefully
- ☐ How to do laundry
- ☐ How to say "No"
- ☐ How to tie three basic knots
- ☐ How to write a great thank-you note
- ☐ How to figure something out on your own
- ☐ How to ask for help
- ☐ How to build a campfire
- ☐ How to journal like a pro
- ☐ How to go after something with gusto
- ☐ How to start a petition
- ☐ How to balance a spoon on your nose
- ☐ How to make a cool craft
- ☐ How to make your bed
- ☐ How to deal with change

- ☐ How to raise money for a good cause
- ☐ How to be worldly
- ☐ How to be disciplined
- ☐ How to handle an emergency
- ☐ How to plant something
- ☐ How to edit a video
- ☐ How to be brave
- ☐ How to express yourself
- ☐ How to read a map
- ☐ How to take care of your teeth
- ☐ How to be truly grateful
- ☐ How to keep your balance
- ☐ How to recover from embarrassment like a champ
- ☐ How to do a card trick
- ☐ How to identify at least one planet
- ☐ How to come up with the perfect secret handshake
- ☐ How to turn an idea into reality
- ☐ How to remember someone's name
- ☐ How to plan a party
- ☐ How to pack a suitcase like a pro
- ☐ How to use a hammer, wrench, and screwdriver
- ☐ How to ace an English test
- ☐ How to identify the 7 continents and 5 oceans on a map or globe
- ☐ How to check out books at your local library

- ☐ How to wrap a present
- ☐ How to take care of a pet
- ☐ How to make comfort food
- ☐ How to improvise in any situation
- ☐ How to throw a softball or baseball
- ☐ How to respectfully disagree
- ☐ How to be resilient
- ☐ How to be a gracious winner and loser
- ☐ How to speak up
- ☐ How to pump up your bike tires
- ☐ How to throw a football
- ☐ How to write a personal story
- ☐ How to manage your money
- ☐ How to press flowers
- ☐ How to study
- ☐ How to have a friend for life
- ☐ How to relax and de-stress
- ☐ How to respond when someone hurts your feelings
- ☐ How to papier mâché
- ☐ How to hit the off button
- ☐ How to talk to adults
- ☐ How to handle yourself online
- ☐ How to impress at a party
- ☐ How to be a critical thinker
- ☐ How to exercise
- ☐ How to be an adventurous eater
- ☐ How to carve a pumpkin
- ☐ How to let your imagination run wild
- ☐ How to build an awesome pillow fort
- ☐ How to start a club
- ☐ How to make new friends
- ☐ How to look on the bright side
- ☐ How to break a bad habit
- ☐ How you can help save the planet
- ☐ Discover where you came from
- ☐ How to decide what you want to be when you grow up
- ☐ How to deal with jealousy
- ☐ How to train a dog to do a trick
- ☐ How to handle a knife safely
- ☐ How to solve problems
- ☐ How to memorize all 50 states
- ☐ How to tell your left from your right
- ☐ How to be tolerant
- ☐ How to quiet your mind
- ☐ How to choose the perfect gift
- ☐ How to take a great yearbook photo
- ☐ How to load the dishwasher
- ☐ How to shine like the star you are
- ☐ How to tell someone you *like* like them
- ☐ How to soothe a burn, beesting, and mosquito bite
- ☐ How to let go of regret
- ☐ How to make yourself happy

INDEX

Find Out More

Grab a parent and visit these websites for more information!

1. fox.com/masterchef-junior
2. thehawnfoundation.org
3. kickstarter.com
4. redcross.org
5. roadtripnation.com

PHOTO CREDITS

Burmakin/SS; 157 (LO), Gianna Stadelmyer/DR; 159 (UP), vlada. marchenko/SS; 159 (CTR), michael baister/AL; 159 (LO CTR), Edwin Remsberg/AL; 159 (LO), Marina Kutukova/SS; 160, Valentyn Volkov/SS; 161 (UP), vasabii/SS; 161 (LO), IS/Tomwang112; 162, IS/christiannpedersen; 164, IS/Charles Mann; 165 (LE), IS/pjohnson1; 165 (RT), IS/claylib; 166-167, De Visu/AL; 168 (UP), Skylines/SS; 168 (LO LE), pukach/SS; 168 (LO RT), Ilya Akinshin/SS; 169 (BACK), STILLFX/SS; 169 (UP), Joshua Davenport/AL; 169 (LO), Sabphoto/SS; 170 (BACK), STILLFX/SS; 170 (UP), Erin Patrice O'Brien/GI; 170 (LO), Just One Film/GI; 171 (UP), Benne Ochs/GI; 171 (LO), David Grossman/AL; 172, Viachaslau Kraskouski/SS; 175, R. Eko Bintoro/DR; 176, BSG/SS; 178, Bernhard Classen/AL; 180 (UP LE), Elena Schweitzer/SS; 180 (UP RT), Alhovik/SS; 180 (UP CTR), koya979/SS; 180 (UP RT and LO RT), koya979/SS; 180-181 (BACK), Silver Spiral Arts/SS; 181, Mukhina Viktoriia/SS; 182, IS/RuslanDashinsky; 183, Jesada Sabai/SS; 184, John Wollwerth/SS; 185 (UP), Vibrant Image Studio/SS; 185 (LO RT), IS/vaeenma; 185 (CTR RT), irin-k/SS; 185 (LE), Eric Isselee/SS; 186 (UP), Gtranquillity/SS; 186 (LO), Oleksiy Maksymenk/AL; 187 (BACK), Oleksiy Maksymenk/AL; 187 (1), Oleksiy Maksymenko/AL; 187 (2), Oleksiy Maksymenko/AL; 187 (3), Oleksiy Maksymenk/AL; 187 (4), Oleksiy Maksymenk/AL; 187 (5), Oleksiy Maksymenk/AL; 187 (CTR), Viktor1/SS; 190, Tim MacPherson/GI; 191, Donald Iain Smith/GI; 192, David

Malan/GI; 193, jupco Smokovski/SS; 194, alapagosPhoto/SS; 195, Blend Images - JGI/Jamie Grill/GI; 196-197 (BACK), panyajampatong/SS; 196-197 (insets), Lyudmyla Kharlamova/SS; 196 (LO LE), Berents/SS; 197 (LO RT), Elnur/SS; 198, IS/Cathy Yeulet; 199, Olesia Bilkei/SS; 200 (UP LE), Kinzie Riehm/GI; 200 (CTR), sarkao/SS; 203, IS/Jodi Matthews; 204, jf/GI; 206, Andrew Bret Wallis/GI; 207, ArtMarie/GI; 208, IS/franckreporter; 213, Sanjida Rashid; 214, Karen Moskowitz/GI; 215, Daniel Grill/GI; 217, Markus Mainka/SS; 218, photocell/SS; 219 (BACK), photocell/SS; 219 (LE), Photoconcepts/Frank and Helena/GI; 219 (RT), IS/Qpicimages; 222, lena Salanovich/SS; 223, IS/

bulentozber; 224, IS/RapidEye; 226, Catalin Petolea/SS; 228, Ditty_about_summer/SS; 229, Kristen Brynelsen; 230, IS/DragonImages; 232, D. Hurst/AL; 233 (UP), UMA Press, Inc/AL; 233 (CTR), ZUMA Press, Inc/AL; 233 (LO), ZUMA Press, Inc/AL; 234, Tiplyashina Evgeniya/SS; 235, Dale & Cathy Irby Collection; 236 (UP), Number1411/SS; 236 (LO), Lonni/SS; 236 (CTR), IS/RapidEye; 237, Deymos.HR/SS; 237 (CTR), Kickstand/iStockphoto; 239, Nyul/DR; 241, IS/DianaHirsch; 242 (LE), IS/Antagain; 242 (RT), IS/Vinicius Ramalh Tupinamba; 243 (RT), IS/Vinicius Ramalh Tupinamba; 243 (LE), alentyn Volkov/SS; 243 (RT), IS/Antagain; 244, Maryna Kordiumova/DR; 246, gulserinak1955/SS

Phew! 100 things is a lot! Bet you're exhausted. Did you keep track of all the different skills you learned in this book by counting the icons? Tally up your totals and show off your score! Go online to natgeo.com/kids/explorer-action-card to print out an official Explorer Action Card to really put your smarts on display. It'll make a great addition to the front of the 'fridge. And just because this book ends doesn't mean the fun has to. For more explorer challenges, tips and tricks, information, fun facts, and activities, visit kids.nationalgeographic.com. After all, this is just the beginning. It's your world—explore it!

CREDITS

STAFF FOR THIS BOOK

Becky Baines, *Project Editor*
Laura Marsh, *Project Manager*
Callie Broaddus, *Art Director and Designer*
Steffan MacMillan, *Designer*
Lori Epstein, *Senior Photo Editor*
Hillary Leo, *Photo Editor*
Debbie Gibbons, *Director of Intracompany and Custom Cartography*
Greg Ugiansky, *Map Research and Production*
Paige Towler, *Editorial Assistant*
Sanjida Rashid and Rachel Kenny, *Design Production Assistants*
Tammi Colleary-Loach, *Rights Clearance Manager*
Michael Cassady and Mari Robinson, *Rights Clearance Specialists*
Grace Hill, *Managing Editor*
Joan Gossett, *Senior Production Editor*
Lewis R. Bassford, *Production Manager*
Jennifer Hoff, *Manager, Production Services*
Susan Borke, *Legal and Business Affairs*

PUBLISHED BY THE NATIONAL GEOGRAPHIC SOCIETY

Gary E. Knell, *President and CEO*
John M. Fahey, *Chairman of the Board*
Melina Gerosa Bellows, *Chief Education Officer*
Declan Moore, *Chief Media Officer*
Hector Sierra, *Senior Vice President and General Manager, Book Division*

SENIOR MANAGEMENT TEAM, KIDS PUBLISHING AND MEDIA

Nancy Laties Feresten, *Senior Vice President*; Erica Green, *Vice President, Editorial Director, Kids Books*; Amanda Larsen, *Design Director, Kids Books*; Jennifer Emmett, *Vice President, Content*; Eva Absher-Schantz, *Vice President, Visual Identity*; Rachel Buchholz, *Editor and Vice President, NG Kids magazine*; Jay Sumner, *Photo Director*; Hannah August, *Marketing Director*; R. Gary Colbert, *Production Director*

DIGITAL
Laura Goertzel, *Manager*; Sara Zeglin, *Senior Producer*; Bianca Bowman, *Assistant Producer*; Natalie Jones, *Senior Product Manager*

The National Geographic Society is one of the world's largest nonprofit scientific and educational organizations. Founded in 1888 to "increase and diffuse geographic knowledge," the Society's mission is to inspire people to care about the planet. It reaches more than 400 million people worldwide each month through its official journal, *National Geographic*, and other magazines; National Geographic Channel; television documentaries; music; radio; films; books; DVDs; maps; exhibitions; live events; school publishing programs; interactive media; and merchandise. National Geographic has funded more than 10,000 scientific research, conservation, and exploration projects and supports an education program promoting geographic literacy.

For more information, please visit nationalgeographic.com, call 1-800-NGS LINE (647-5463), or write to the following address:
National Geographic Society
1145 17th Street N.W.
Washington, D.C. 20036-4688 U.S.A.
Visit us online at nationalgeographic.com/books

For librarians and teachers: ngchildrensbooks.org

More for kids from National Geographic: natgeokids.com

For information about special discounts for bulk purchases, please contact National Geographic Books Special Sales: ngspecsales@ngs.org

For rights or permissions inquiries, please contact National Geographic Books Subsidiary Rights: ngbookrights@ngs.org

Paperback ISBN: 978-1-4263-2316-4
Reinforced library binding ISBN: 978-1-4263-2317-1

Printed in China

15/PPS/1

NOTE TO PARENTS AND EDUCATORS:

The National Geographic Learning Framework explains what readers will learn from their experiences with our books, products, and other resources. Created to support educators, parents, and families, the Learning Framework shows the ways in which we are dedicated to teaching kids about the world and how it works. If we work together to equip future generations with Attitudes and Skills—woven through critical Knowledge areas—that embody the attributes of explorers, the learning process extends beyond the page or screen and can shape real-world experiences. For more information, check out page 5 and go to NatGeoEd.org/learningframework.